The Little Book of Insider Dealing

Gregory Durston and Mohsin Zaidi

❈ WATERSIDE PRESS

ISBN 978-1-909976-53-5 (Paperback)
ISBN 978-1-910979-51-8 (Epub E-book)
ISBN 978-1-910979-52-5 (Adobe E-book)

Cover design © 2018 Waterside Press by www.gibgob.com

Printed by Lightning Source.

Main UK distributor Gardners Books, 1 Whittle Drive, Eastbourne, East Sussex, BN23 6QH. Tel: +44 (0)1323 521777; sales@gardners.com; www.gardners.com

North American distribution Ingram Book Company, One Ingram Blvd, La Vergne, TN 37086, USA. Tel: (+1) 615 793 5000; inquiry@ingramcontent.com

Cataloguing-In-Publication Data A catalogue record for this book can be obtained from the British Library.

e-book *The Little Book of Insider Dealing* is available as an ebook and also to subscribers of Ebrary, Ebsco, Myilibrary and Dawsonera.

Published 2018 by
Waterside Press Ltd
Sherfield Gables
Sherfield on Loddon, Hook
Hampshire RG27 0JG.

Telephone +44(0)1256 882250
Online catalogue WatersidePress.co.uk
Email enquiries@watersidepress.co.uk

Contents

6. **Evidential Perspectives** **115**

7. **FSA/FCA Prosecutions** **135**

Publisher's note

The views and opinions expressed in this book are those of the authors entirely and are not necessarily shared by the publisher. Readers should draw their own conclusions about any claims made or any facts or opinions stated in the book concerning which the possibility of alternative interpretations, narratives, descriptions, subtleties of terminology or developments not sufficiently reported or in the public domain at the time of writing, or which may have occurred since that time should be borne in mind.

Acknowledgements

We would like to acknowledge the invaluable assistance provided by the staff at Kingston University Library, Lincoln's Inn Library, the London School of Economics Library, the Bodleian Law Library, University of Monaco Library and the British Library. Additionally, we are extremely grateful for advice and assistance from Judge Nicholas Philpot, Victor Temple QC, and Philippa Russell. Readers should note that abbreviated titles are sometimes used in footnotes; the full versions of these sources can be found in the *Select Bibliography*. Some newspaper citations refer to electronic editions.

Gregory Durston
Mohsin Zaidi

London, January 2018

About the authors

Gregory Durston is a barrister-at-law who has taught in Law Schools in England and Japan. He was Reader in Law at Kingston University, Surrey and is the author of *Whores and Highwaymen: Crime and Justice in the Eighteenth-Century Metropolis* (Waterside Press, hardback 2012; paperback 2016) and *Fields, Fens and Felonies: Crime and Justice in Eighteenth-Century East Anglia* (Waterside Press, 2016).

Mohsin Zaidi is a barrister in practice at 6KBW College Hill specialising in corporate crime and investigations. Before transferring to the Bar, he was a solicitor at Linklaters LLP where he worked on a number of complex and high profile matters, including major investigations into FTSE 100 companies and financial institutions. In 2013, he was appointed judicial assistant to Lords Sumption and Wilson at the Supreme Court of the United Kingdom. He is a member of the Serious Fraud Office Prosecutions C Panel and also of the New York Bar. Mohsin read Law with European Law at Keble College, Oxford University and thereafter worked as a research assistant to an academic at Harvard Kennedy School of Government.

CHAPTER 1

Introduction

Setting the Scene

A front page headline of *The Times* newspaper recently announced 'City traders getting away with abuse of markets—insider deals by white-collar criminals ignored'.[1] This timely and concise work aims to provide the reader, whether student, professional or interested member of the public, with a brief introduction to the crime of insider dealing (or 'trading' as it is often termed, especially in the USA) within the UK, with particular reference to England and Wales, and with a special focus on the evidential problems raised by such cases. It is not a substitute for the leading practitioner texts on the subject (on which it has drawn) or for reading the relevant cases (where they have been reported) and Statutes.[2] It has been written to provide a reasoned analysis of the subject, accompanied by comments and references to stimulate further study. The book concentrates on the issues posed by typical offences that come to trial, rather than on the crime's more

---

1   *The Times*, 19 January 2018.

2   Such as Sarah Clarke's magisterial and specialist *Insider Dealing: Law and Practice*, Oxford University Press, 2013. Barry Rider *et al*, *Market Abuse and Insider Dealing*, Bloomsbury Professional, 2016 is also a valuable study of all areas of the field. Karen Anderson *et al, A Practitioner's Guide to the Law and Regulation of Market Abuse*, Sweet & Maxwell, 2017 is the most recent, and detailed, general publication on this topic at the time of going to press in February 2018. Paul Barnes' *Stock Market Efficiency, Insider Dealing and Market Abuse*, Routledge, 2009, which has a much heavier focus on economic and financial matters, is also well worth reading.

theoretical and recondite aspects. Nevertheless, to make sense of the topic, its prevalence, history, the rationale for its existence and its close relationship to (civil) regulatory actions for insider dealing are also considered. Before going further a general description of terms is necessary.

One of the most important markets in which insider dealing occurs in the UK is that relating to shares traded on the London Stock Exchange (LSE). However, as will be seen, many other markets, both at home and abroad, are also covered by the current UK criminal regime. If investors in these markets slowly become aware that a company listed on them is doing very well or, conversely, is in serious difficulties, its share price will gradually rise or fall to reflect this. By contrast, the public announcement of previously unexpected news, whether good or bad, can occasion sudden major price movements in a company's shares. UK companies that are publicly listed are obliged to publish price-sensitive information that affects them through a Regulatory Information Service (an approved newswire service), such as the LSE's own Regulatory News Service (RNS), in an expeditious manner. Once published, investors and the media will quickly pick up the information and react accordingly.

Typically, a takeover bid might push up the share price of a company, because the bidders will almost invariably have to offer a relatively high price to persuade the owners of shares to part with their holdings. Conversely, profits warnings of unexpectedly bad results will drive the share price down. ('Short-selling' and spread-betting, *inter alia*, allow investors to make a profit on a share's fall).[3] These are easily the two most common causes of sudden share volatility, and so of insider dealing. For example, in *R v Asif Nazir Butt* [2006] 2 Cr App R (S) 44, 19 transactions conducted over more than three years formed the basis of the allegation of insider dealing. They were allegedly founded on information gleaned from the defendant's work in the Compliance Control Room of a major bank, something that gave him access to confidential information relating to the status of companies that the bank was advising. Seven of the deals involved advance knowledge of profits warnings by companies that had done worse than expected while

---

3   Paul Barnes, *Stock Market Efficiency, Insider Dealing and Market Abuse*, 2009, p.11.

12

12 concerned confidential information regarding takeover bids. The latter phenomenon has become particularly important because of the huge growth in takeover activity over the past two decades.[4] By way of illustration, at the end of 2016, news that the broadcaster Sky had agreed to an £11.2 billion takeover by 21st Century Fox saw the former's shares increased in value by almost 30 per cent within an hour.[5]

Nevertheless, there are many other possible pieces of news that might have the same effect on share value, such as an armaments company winning (or losing) an important government contract to supply warplanes or tanks, a shipbuilding company getting a substantial order, a gold mining company suddenly discovering a huge seam of precious metal, the success or failure of a pharmaceutical company's new 'wonder drug', or the purchase or sale of a large tranche of shares in a specific company by a major institutional investor.

As the case of *Butt* (mentioned above and see also in later chapters) suggests, there are always people in or working for a company, whether directors, employees, professional advisers (internal or external), lawyers and accountants, or even inquisitive support staff (like secretaries and printroom workers), who know of this type of price-sensitive information well before it is made public. If one of them buys or sells shares, whether personally or through a third party, or passes on information to an associate who does so (knowing that it has come from an inside source), usually in practice with a view to making a profit or avoiding a loss,[6] insider dealing takes place. Buying or selling shares in anticipation of a major institutional purchase or disposal of the same equities (which will affect their price) is sufficiently common to have acquired its own term, 'front running', and often involves dealing by the employee of a financial adviser who has work-acquired advance knowledge of a large forthcoming transaction in those equities.[7]

---

4   Barry Rider *et al, Market Abuse and Insider Dealing*, 2016, p.43.

5   *Financial Times*, 9 December 2016.

6   Though neither is an essential ingredient in establishing a *prima facie* 'case to answer': see *Chapter 4*; even if the absence of anticipated profit or loss may, in prescribed circumstances, be a statutory defence in criminal proceedings: see *Chapter 5*.

7   Paul Barnes, 'Insider Dealing and Market Abuse: The UK's Record on Enforcement', 2011, p.178.

In the modern era, it is not even necessary to buy the shares themselves to take advantage of such information, as various financial derivatives, such as contracts for difference (CFD) and options, can be purchased, which leverage the effects of movement in the price of a stock.[8] Although reference will often be made to shares in this book, it must be remembered that the legislation covers many other securities.

The sequence of events that led to the conviction of Ryan Willmott, the financial planning manager of Logica PLC (the takeover of which gave rise to several entirely separate insider dealing cases), provides a simple illustration of the commission of a relatively small-scale example of such a crime.

R v Ryan Willmott

On 19 April 2012, Ryan Willmott learned of the imminent takeover of his employer, Logica, where he was Head of Financial Planning, by a Canadian company called CGI. On the evening of 28 May 2012 the accused visited a family friend at his house and provided him with this information. On the morning of 29 May 2012, within the first ten minutes of the LSE opening, the friend liquidated all of his other trading positions so that he could use the funds released to purchase 62,000 Logica shares (both on his own and Willmott's behalf), at a price of 68.5 pence per share, using his online trading account. Willmott also set up an online Natwest stockbrokers account under his former girlfriend's name (without her knowledge). He invested his entire £10,000 savings in Logica shares via this account.

Two days later, at seven am on 31 May 2012, CGI publicly announced the agreement of a recommended cash acquisition of the entire share capital of Logica (a £1.7 billion takeover). The price of Logica shares immediately rose from 65.7 pence to 105 pence. Just over an hour later, on the same day, the friend sold all of his Logica shares in two tranches.[9] Willmott's own (direct) investment increased to more than £16,000 in value.

Wilmott was subsequently prosecuted for the criminal offence of insider dealing. In early 2015, he pleaded guilty and was imprisoned for ten months, while his friend (who had co-operated with the regulator and been uncertain

---

8   Paul Barnes, *Stock Market Efficiency, Insider Dealing and Market Abuse*, 2009, p.19.

9   FCA Final Notice (i.e. to the family friend), 30 March 2015.

of the legal status of the information when he traded) was dealt with under the civil regulatory provisions for market abuse, then contained in section 118(2) of the Financial Services and Markets Act (FSMA) 2000 (now found in Article 14 Market Abuse Regulation (MAR)).[10]

Other jurisdictions

Precisely what behaviour constitutes insider dealing varies considerably between jurisdictions and, occasionally, even between regulatory and criminal proceedings in the same country, although this is not necessarily the situation in the UK (where there is a substantial, but not total, overlap). For example, there are major differences between the enforcement regimes found on either side of the Atlantic.

The USA, unlike the UK, does not adopt a general 'parity of information' approach, whereby dealers cannot normally trade on price-sensitive information that is not publicly available. In America, the law usually prohibits dealing on non-public information only when it has been wrongfully obtained or used.[11] Indeed, the regulatory models used to deal with insider dealing are traditionally divided in two to reflect this systemic difference: the 'fiduciary' approach, whose main example is the American system, and the 'market protection' approach, which can be found in countries in the European Union.[12] Two of the highest regulatory fines for insider dealing imposed in England involved foreign nationals (one of them American) who, apparently, believed that they were acting entirely lawfully.[13] The UK regime does not require any breach of an obligation of confidentiality or fiduciary duty, merely 'asymmetric access' to inside information that gives the dealer an unfair advantage over third parties who do not have such knowledge.[14] This book focuses exclusively on the position in the UK.

---

10   Ibid; *Daily Telegraph*, 26 February 2015.

11   John C Coffee, 'How to Get Away With Insider Trading', *New York Times*, 23 May 2016.

12   Carmen Estevan de Quesada, 'Regulatory Models of Insider Trading and the Concept of "Use of Inside Information"', 2014, p.169.

13   *Financial Times*, 27 January 2012.

14   Karen Anderson *et al, A Practitioner's Guide to the Law and Regulation of Market Abuse*, 2017, p.12.

Rationale for Proscription

Insider dealing is proscribed because it undermines trust in the market and the existence of a 'level playing field' for all investors. It is often suggested that, ideally, the stock exchange would be a 'pure' or 'efficient' market, where everybody has access to the same information at exactly the same time (which is why the LSE requires that very important company announcements be made through its own information service). In theory, the only permissible inequalities would arise from the various participants' abilities to analyse the information. Of course, in reality, a professional dealer who is permanently wired-up to his or her computer console is likely to notice and react to such information very much faster than, for example, a technophobic amateur investor who is dependent on printed media. Nevertheless, the theory is clear.

As a result of such views, and as Lord Lane noted many years ago, in the modern era insider dealing is usually viewed as a form of 'cheating'.[15] More recently, when sentencing one person who had been convicted of insider dealing in December 2016, His Honour Judge Goymer reportedly observed that: 'Insider dealing is not a victimless crime, I regard these offences as premeditated and blatantly dishonest'.[16] In simple terms, it means that uninformed investors pay more than they should when they buy shares and get less than they otherwise would when they sell them.[17] More generally, it is thought that insider dealing undermines modern attempts at creating what, in the 1980s, was referred to as a 'shareholder democracy', something that was expressly encouraged by the then Government allowing individuals to purchase small numbers of shares on favourable terms when publicly owned utilities were privatised. This requires that ordinary (i.e. non-institutional or specialist) investors have confidence in the market in which they place their money, and are able to operate in an environment that is not contaminated by those holding the equivalent of 'marked' cards.

---

15   *Attorney-General's Reference (No 1 of 1988)* [1989] 2 WLR 729.

16   *FT Adviser,* 22 December 2016.

17   Paul Barnes, *Stock Market Efficiency, Insider Dealing and Market Abuse,* 2009, p.10.

Arguments for legalised insider dealing

Nevertheless, arguments for legalised insider dealing (fiduciaries apart) are still sometimes made, on the basis that it performs a valuable function in allowing share prices to adjust to levels that reflect an issuing company's underlying fundamentals, rather than what its officers say about them in public. This argument, first made by Professor Henry Manne in the 1960s in his controversial article 'In Defense of Insider Trading', has been restated more recently.[18] For example, in 2003, Milton Friedman suggested that making the practice illegal drove it underground, whilst an openly transparent system would lead to greater information sharing: 'You want more insider dealing, not less. You want to give people most likely to have knowledge about deficiencies of the company an incentive to make the public aware of that'.[19] Donald Boudreaux, an economics professor at George Mason University, has reiterated this analysis, suggesting that: 'Far from being so injurious to the economy that its practice must be criminalized, insiders buying and selling stocks based on their knowledge play a critical role in keeping asset prices honest — in keeping prices from lying to the public about corporate realities'.[20] In 1986, Sir Martin Jacomb, a distinguished banker, went so far as to suggest that insider dealing was a 'victimless crime', although, as some of the judicial quotations cited above suggest, this is a view that has been expressly, and regularly, rejected by the higher courts in England and Wales.[21]

The presence of such attitudes probably contributes to more widespread notions of insider dealing not being 'truly' criminal and may help to explain the willingness of some professional people to break the criminal law in this regard. It may also help to explain why a significant number of convictions for insider dealing in recent years have been secured by a majority verdict.

Historical Context

There is a long history behind the use of the criminal law to regulate English markets, as can be seen from the Act Against Regrators, Forestallers

---

18   Jonathan Macey, 'Securities Trading: A Contractual Perspective', 1999, pp.269–272.

19   *Daily Telegraph*, 10 June 2009.

20   Opinion Piece in *The Wall Street Journal*, 24 October 2009.

21   *Evening Standard*, 15 March 2010; *Financial Times*, 10 July 2007.

and Engrossers of 1552. Despite this, insider dealing was a late arrival in the criminal canon. This was not because it is a recent phenomenon. It is as old as stock markets. In 1687, Nicolaas Muys van Holy, an Amsterdam lawyer, published a book arguing against speculation on the city's (relatively) new stock exchange. One of his targets was trading by Dutch East India Company directors and political leaders who were privy to inside information. The following year, Joseph De la Vega argued that mechanisms for making transactions more transparent must be introduced, in part to avoid the insider trading that was all too frequent on the Amsterdam market, especially that conducted by (again) East India Company directors.[22]

Despite this history, the American legal academic and evidence scholar H L Wilgus made the first carefully articulated case against insider trading in an article published as late as 1910. He thought that it discouraged investment in the stock market and offended the 'moral sense'.[23] Other prominent legal academics, such as Professor A A Berle (1895–1971), agreed with his analysis and supported Wilgus' desire to outlaw the practice. It was eventually made a crime in the USA by section 10(b) of the Securities Exchange Act of 1934, long before it was criminalised elsewhere in the world. In part, this may have been because it was a more serious problem in America than in the UK and other Anglophone countries at this time. The advent of the new crime was partly prompted by the behaviour of men such as Albert Wiggin, the head of Chase National Bank during the Depression, who made a practice of short-selling shares in his own company on inside information, making over $4,000,000 in the process, without committing an offence.[24]

Insider dealing has only been a crime in the UK since 1980 and a civil wrong since 2000. As a result, English company directors could deal using inside information with relative impunity until well into the 20th-century. As late as 1902, Mr Justice Swindon Eady held that directors who bought and sold the shares of their company whilst in possession of what would now

---

22 Herve Dumez, 'The Description of the First Financial Market: Looking back on Confusion of confusions by Joseph de la Vega', 2016, pp.5–9.

23 H L Wilgus, 'Purchase of Shares of Corporation by a Director from a Shareholder', 1910, 8 Mich. L. Rev. 267.

24 *New York Times*, 22 May 1951.

be termed 'price-sensitive' information' owed no fiduciary duty to disclose this to other parties to the transaction: *Percival v Wright* (1902) 2 CH 421. They only owed duties of loyalty to the company.

Perhaps unsurprisingly, there is some evidence of suspicious increases in share price in late-Victorian and Edwardian companies during the weeks before a dividend increase was announced (and vice-versa). Nevertheless, using this as an (imperfect) indicator, it seems that the level of insider dealing at this time was *relatively* modest, despite the lack of formal regulation. It may have been curbed by social norms, a general feeling that it was 'bad form', the personal nature of shareholding during the era, and the close proximity of directors to shareholders. More cynically, it could have been because there were far more efficient ways to make money fraudulently from publicly listed companies.[25]

Whatever the situation may have been around 1900, for much of the 20th-century insider dealing appears to have been widespread in The Square Mile, frequently conducted by company directors, officers, or professional advisers, and almost considered legitimate activity, although it should be noted that the Marconi insider dealing scandal of 1912 rocked British society to its foundations. Senior members of the cabinet, including David Lloyd George and the about to be appointed Attorney-General Sir Rufus Isaacs, speculated in shares in Marconi shortly before it was made public that the company had (as they knew) been selected to provide the Imperial Wireless Chain.[26] Even so, that stockbrokers were thought to have superior access to price-sensitive information was one reason that ordinary people employed them, rather than making investment decisions themselves.[27]

A Company Law Reform Committee (the Cohen Committee), established in 1943 to modernise company law, discussed insider dealing as a form of malpractice in its report of 1945. The committee concluded that directors' dealings based on privileged information were 'clearly improper'. Even so,

25 F.Braggion and L Moore, 'How Insiders Traded Before Rules', 2013, pp.565–584. F. Braggion and L. Moore, 'How Insiders Traded Before Rules', Centre Discussion Paper Series No. 2012–0, University of Southampton.

26 A N Wilson, *Hilaire Belloc*, Penguin, Harmondsworth, 1984, pp.192–200.

27 Paul Thompson, 'The Pyrrhic Victory of Gentlemanly Capitalism: The Financial Elite of the City of London, 1945–90. Part 2', 1997, p.80.

witnesses giving evidence before them suggested that insider dealing was endemic within the LSE. Little changed over ensuing decades. The head of the LSE's insider dealing group told a 1990 Select Committee that buyers traditionally went: '... to the broker who had the best information, and that information would be inside'. The long City lunches of the era facilitated the transmission of such information.

However, although widespread and even tacitly accepted, insider dealing was not overtly condoned after the Great War and, between the end of the Second World War and the late-1950s, was increasingly considered unethical and improper.[28] The Jenkins Committee on Company Law, established in 1959, which considered, *inter alia*, directors' duties, also concluded in its 1962 report that it was wrong, albeit that much of the evidence that it received, from a variety of sources, including the Board of Trade, was quite pessimistic about how readily it could be sanctioned, not least because directors with inside information could buy or sell shares through nominees.[29] Even so, the report's recommendation that directors be prohibited from dealing in options in their own companies was followed by the enactment of section 25 of the Companies Act 1967.

Nevertheless, there were several attempts to prevent insider dealing by 'self-regulation' prior to criminalisation, both by the LSE and the City Panel on Mergers and Takeovers, some of which invoked a power to suspend dealers from the Exchange. The Takeover Panel was the primary regulator for insider dealing for about ten years. Its first internal investigation, in 1971, resulted in a public censure being administered to the culprit and, from 1975 onwards, culpable dealers started to donate their illicit profits to charities at the behest of the panel.[30] Even so, such measures were not felt to be adequate.

In 1972, Lord Shawcross, a former Attorney-General, was one of several prominent observers who called for the practice to be made a criminal offence.[31] In a report the same year, the British section of the International

---

28 H H Marshall, *Insider Trading*, 1978, pp.250–252.

29 Barry Rider *et al*, *The Regulation of Insider Trading*, 1979, pp.191–192.

30 Jack Davies, 'From Gentlemanly Expectations to Regulatory Principles: A History of Insider Dealing in the UK: Part 1', 2015, p.142.

31 *The Times*, 23 September 1972.

Commission of Jurists recommended that: '... insider trading through a Stock exchange (but not outside it) should be made a specific criminal offence'.[32] At about the same time, the LSE's chairman claimed that insider dealing was 'no better than theft'.[33] In 1973, the Stock Exchange and the Takeover Panel issued a joint statement calling for the introduction of criminal sanctions for the practice. Even so, two legislative proposals to deal with the problem were abandoned during the 1970s (in 1973 and 1978) if only because the Governments sponsoring the bills lost ensuing elections. Success was finally achieved just after the end of that decade, the new provisions, set out in sections 68 to 73 of the Companies Act 1980, coming into force in June of the same year and introducing 12 offences of 'primary' and 'secondary' insider dealing.[34]

It should be noted that, although well behind the USA in introducing such legislation, the UK was not particularly slow by much international comparison, especially when it came to jurisdictions in Continental Europe. Although France was relatively early when introducing statutory controls on insider dealing in 1970, Germany did not outlaw the practice until 1994, only doing so after the EU required it in the European Community's Insider Dealing Directive of November 1989, despite it being a long acknowledged problem in that country.[35] Germany's apparent tardiness was not exceptional. At the start of the 1990s, insider trading was not illegal in most European countries.[36] Italy, Belgium, and several other Continental countries also only introduced such a regime after the 1989 directive came into force. Moving continent, it was not until 1988 that Japan passed its first insider trading law, violation of which carries a maximum sentence of three years in prison. Even so, in 2010, Japanese investors were still claiming that a blind-eye was being turned to insider dealing, with favoured investors being let in on price-sensitive information.[37]

---

32   William Goodhart *et al, Insider Trading: A Report by Justice,* 1972, p.11.

33   *The Times,* 23 November 1972.

34   Jack Davies, 'From Gentlemanly Expectations to Regulatory Principles: A History of Insider Dealing in the UK: Part 1', 2015, p.132.

35   89/592/EEC, 13 November 1989.

36   Utpal Bhattacharya and Hazem Daouk, 'The World Price of Insider Trading', 2002, p.75.

37   *The Times,* 24 September 2010.

Some common law jurisdictions were also slower than the UK in introducing legislation. Although Canada passed its first insider trading laws in 1966, and Australia in 1970, in Hong Kong, insider dealing was only made a criminal offence as late as 2003 (albeit that it had almost become one in 1974), and there were no prosecutions for the crime until 2008. Considering the globe as a whole, prior to 1990, of 103 nations studied worldwide, only 34 had anti-insider trading laws; even more significantly, just nine of them had actually prosecuted cases. However, these figures had risen to 87 and 38 respectively by 2002.[38]

Insider dealing is now prohibited in almost all developed countries. Despite this, there is a major divergence in the frequency with which sanctions (of all types) are imposed for such trading around the world. For example, after comparing sanctions to the size of market capitalisation, the UK was significantly ahead of Hong Kong, slightly ahead of the province of Ontario in Canada, but well behind the USA, Australia, and (the leader in sanctioning insider dealing) Singapore.[39] Of course, it is not necessarily an equal problem in all of these markets, and some sanctions are much milder than others.

Perhaps a little unfairly, given its pioneering role, the Companies Act 1980 was widely seen as a failure. Convictions were usually the result of guilty pleas in straightforward cases, rather than being secured after contested hearings involving complex allegations, and they attracted moderate punishments. For example, in August 1981, the first conviction under the new Act was secured in Scotland by the Lord Advocate (the chief legal officer of the Crown in that jurisdiction), rather than by the Department of Trade and Industry (DTI), which conducted most English investigations into insider dealing at this time. An investment manager was prosecuted for insider dealing and pleaded guilty. He was censured, had to relinquish his profit from the trade, but then given an absolute discharge.[40]

The first successful DTI prosecution, which occurred the following year,

---

38   Utpal Bhattacharya and Hazem Daouk, 'The World Price of Insider Trading', 2002, p.76.

39   Lev Bromberg *et al*, 'The Extent and Intensity of Insider Trading Enforcement — An International Comparison', 2017, p.14.

40   Paul Barnes, *Stock Market Efficiency, Insider Dealing and Market Abuse*, 2009, p.158.

involved the secretary of a merchant banker who divulged inside information concerning the takeover of Joseph Stocks & Sons to her husband, who then purchased shares in the company. Both husband and wife pleaded guilty and were each fined £4,000. As they retained illicit profits of over £6,000, each fine was less than £1,000 in real terms. The second successful case from 1982 was equally straightforward. A managing director who had purchased an options contract as a result of inside information pleaded guilty to the crime. He received a suspended six-month prison sentence.[41]

The DTI faced considerable difficulties when defendants pleaded 'not guilty'. In the first contested case two stockbrokers, who had allegedly received inside information from a client, were acquitted, as the trial judge was not convinced that they knew the information was from an 'inside' source. During the first five years of the criminal regime initiated by the 1980 Act the DTI concluded 12 investigations. However, these produced only seven prosecutions and resulted in just three convictions (including guilty pleas).[42]

In part as a result of this apparent lack of success, insider dealing received its own legislation in the Company Securities (Insider Dealing) Act 1985. However, the new Statute made only minor revisions to the previous regime. As with its predecessor, comparatively few successful prosecutions were brought under the new Act.[43] For example, in 1992, in *R v Gray* (1995) 2 Cr App R 100, the appellants (two merchant bankers, an investment analyst and a fund manager) were convicted of offences under the 1985 Act after a seven-week trial. It was alleged that they passed information that they had acquired from their work to each other, with regard to three companies, using it to make money or, as they allegedly termed it, 'personal spice'. However, all the convictions were quashed on appeal, as the higher court concluded that the trial judge had misdirected the jury as to the use that could be made of evidence relating to a count that had been dismissed after

---

41 Jack Davies, 'From Gentlemanly Expectations to Regulatory Principles: A History of Insider Dealing in the UK, Part 2,' 2015, pp.163–164.

42 Ibid', pp.163–164.

43 Karen Harrison and Nicholas Ryder, *The Law Relating to Financial Crime in the United Kingdom*, 2013, p.99.

a submission of no case to answer, as well as the uses that could be made of recorded conversations and other evidence.[44]

In total, there were 29 trials for insider dealing between 1985 and 1994, involving 46 people. Of these, 19 were found guilty, while 27 were acquitted. Although the maximum penalty under the Act was seven years and/or an unlimited fine (as it is today) only one person was sent to prison, and only a few were given (short) suspended sentences. In 1994, in a case involving shares in Aaronson Brothers, the two defendants were fined just £1,500 each.[45] This is not totally surprising for a newly criminalised offence. In 1972, although the International Commission of Jurists had recommended that insider dealing be a crime punished by imprisonment or fine, they had also observed: 'No doubt a fine would be the usual penalty'.[46]

Many cases that were investigated under the 1985 Act did not proceed any further. For example, on 12th January 1994 the directors of Anglia Television received a takeover bid for their company. The following day, Jeffrey Archer bought 25,000 Anglia shares on behalf of a friend. On 18 January a takeover deal was publicly confirmed, and Archer sold the shares two hours later. His wife, Mary, was a non-executive director of Anglia Television at the time. This attracted a great deal of publicity. Even so, a seven-month long investigation by two outside investigators appointed by the DTI, after it had been alerted to the deal by the LSE, firmly concluded that there was insufficient evidence to establish that any offence had been committed.[47] It should be stressed that both Jeffrey and Mary Archer vehemently denied any wrongdoing and there were wholly legitimate explanations for what had occurred. Nevertheless, even if entirely unfairly, cases like this one attracted popular criticism of the then law and enforcement regime.

As a result, the second attempt to criminalise insider dealing, like the first, was thought to have been disappointing. In early-1994, a government spokesman in the House of Lords suggested that, taking the 1980 and 1985 Acts together, convictions had only been returned against 23 of the 52

---

44   See also *The Times*, 5 August 1994; *The Times*, 10 June 1992.

45   *The Independent*, 9 July 1994.

46   William Goodhart *et al*, *Insider Trading: A Report by Justice*, 1972, p.11.

47   *The Guardian*, 30 October 1999.

individuals who had been prosecuted since insider dealing became a criminal offence, and that many investigations had not even produced indictments.[48] Another effort was thought necessary, especially as it was needed to reflect the new obligations contained in the Insider Dealing Directive of November 1989, the first EU attempt at regulating this form of activity. This eventually produced the criminal regime that is still in force in the UK today, many of whose provisions reflect those of the 1989 directive.

The current crimes and their interpretation are set out in the 13 sections of Part V of the Criminal Justice Act (CJA) 1993, which came into force in February 1994. When introduced, it was hoped that the formulation of just three offences under the new Statute — replacing 12 crimes under the old Company Securities (Insider Dealing) Act 1985 — would make it easier to draft a readily comprehensible indictment and then to present it to a jury. In turn, this would make insider dealing slightly less difficult to prosecute than it had been under its two statutory predecessors.[49] These offences are considered in detail in *Chapter 4* and the relevant parts of Part V of the 1993 Act, as amended, is reproduced in the *Appendix* to this work.

Extent of Insider Dealing in the 21st-Century

The Financial Conduct Authority (FCA), the current regulator, believes that both professional insider dealing rings and rogue individuals who trade using inside information operate in the City of London and elsewhere in the UK. A decade ago, its predecessor, the Financial Services Authority (FSA) conducted research that suggested that insider dealing was widespread, despite major efforts to reduce it.[50] The following year, the FSA's second market cleanliness report identified share price movements (suggesting its presence) shortly before nearly 24 per cent of all takeover announcements made in 2005.[51] Some studies, using a much wider 'window', such as the two months prior to an important announcement, suggest there were significant

---

48 Keith Wotherspoon, 'Insider Dealing: The New Law: Part V of the Criminal Justice Act 1993', 1994, p.433; Iwona Seredyńska, *Insider Dealing and Criminal Law: Dangerous Liaisons*, 2012, p.4.

49 Ibid, Keith Wotherspoon, 'Insider Dealing: The New Law: Part V of the Criminal Justice Act 1993', 1994, p.433.

50 Ben Dubow and Nuno Monteiro, *Measuring Market Cleanliness*, 2006, p.26.

51 Speech by Margaret Cole to the American Bar Association, 4 October 2007.

price movements in more than 90 per cent of cases.[52] Others would argue that at least some of these are explained by quite legitimate market factors.

Nobody seeks to make uninformed investment choices; dealers are constantly, and quite legitimately, searching for relevant information. As a result, The Square Mile is an environment in which gossip flourishes, something that sometimes forces companies to make formal announcements early, simply to bring an end to speculation that is driving share prices up or down (which may or may not be linked to insider dealing). Information has a tendency to 'get out'. This is not entirely surprising. Major takeovers (for example) usually take many weeks of work by a large variety and number of company officers, professionals such as lawyers and accountants (internal and external) and support staff. As is regularly noted, in such an environment 'Chinese walls cannot prevent Chinese whispers'. It has even been claimed that the CIA asked the FSA to help investigate an apparent short-selling of shares in airlines and insurance companies just before the 9/11 terrorist attacks.[53] Perhaps more pertinently, in an insider dealing case from 2010 evidence was received from a former *Financial Times* journalist, who had written about a takeover. The report, which contained the offer price and offering company, had been printed on the morning of the formal announcement. This suggests that the paper had information about the deal before it was publicly released (there was absolutely no suggestion of any impropriety on the part of the journalists). This leak was potentially relevant to the case, and in particular to the issue of whether the information was already public when two of the defendants traded in the days prior to the takeover bid.[54]

Rumours based on multiple-hearsay are sometimes 'in the air', without anyone fully knowing where they originally came from or, more particularly, whether it was an insider leak, legitimate market research and inference, an informed guess, or idle speculation. This state of affairs is captured by a frequently reiterated, if rather cynical, saying in The Square Mile: 'His

---

52 Paul Barnes, 'Insider Dealing and Market Abuse: The UK's Record on Enforcement', 2011, pp.174–189.

53 *The Sunday Times*, 18 September 2001.

54 *New Law Journal*, 3 September 2010.

dealing is based on inside information, yours on rumour, mine on market analysis'. Indeed, the sheer amount of gossip allows other forms of market abuse (to insider dealing) to flourish, these matters also being dealt with by the FCA. For example, dishonest investors may engage in 'share ramping' by broadcasting information that will positively affect a company's share price on an Internet chatroom or notice board, even if it is completely untrue. The fraudster can then make a profit by selling at the inflated price created by the rumour, before it slips back when the mistake is appreciated (this is a criminal offence under section 89 of the Financial Services Act 2012).[55] In these circumstances proving that transactions based on such gossip are insider deals is often almost impossible.

Even so, recent years have seen a significant improvement in 'market cleanliness', albeit an uneven one. In 2011, suspicious trading ahead of UK mergers and acquisitions fell by nearly a third to 21 per cent, the lowest level for eight years.[56] In 2012, the FSA calculated that abnormal share price movements had preceded almost one in five major company announcements the previous year during the two days prior to the news being made public (i.e. ignoring older movements). Nevertheless, this was still a modest improvement on the previous year, and the lowest since 2003.[57] In 2015, the FCA concluded that the incidence of insider trading and market abuse had continued to fall over the ensuing four years.[58] The reasons for this decline are considered further in *Chapter 7*. This might be right, but a two-year long investigation by *The Times* (concluded early in 2018) found that many white-collar criminals were still acting with relative impunity, with inadequate steps being taken to prevent stock market abuse despite research suggesting the system was being exploited.[59] The newspaper analysed share price movements on the day before every major profit warning and every merger or acquisition announcement over a two year period. It found that, on the day before a profit warning, the share price of the company that

---

55   Paul Barnes, 'Insider Dealing and Market Abuse: The UK's Record on Enforcement', 2011, pp.174–189.

56   Jonathan Barnard, 'Insider Trading: An Easy Offence to Commit', 2011, p.4.

57   *The Times*, 20 June 2012.

58   *Daily Telegraph*, 2 July 2015.

59   *The Times*, 19 January 2018.

issued the warning fell in 67 per cent of cases, suggesting that a number of investors were offloading shares in advance of the bad news, potentially saving tens of millions of pounds. Relatedly, the investigation found that on the day before a takeover announcement, the share price increased in 70 per cent of cases which, according to the newspaper, suggests that investors were buying in advance of good news. By contrast, the investigation found that the number of prosecutions for the crime of insider dealing might, in part, be low because identifying and investigating insider dealing is a complex undertaking requiring significant resource. It is this issue that the next chapter seeks to address.

CHAPTER 2

Identifying and Investigating Insider Dealing

Identifying Insider Dealing

Detecting cases of insider dealing is inherently challenging. A vast number of stocks, shares, securities, and derivatives can be purchased and sold and there are numerous regulated forums and markets in which this is done. A huge amount of transactions take place every day. Even so, such trading is exposed on a fairly regular basis, via a variety of mechanisms.

Whistle-blowing and broker observation

Private whistle-blowing reveals a few cases each year, although this appears to be far more common in the USA than in the UK. The Securities and Exchange Commission (SEC) in America is permitted to pay bounties to informants, provided he or she is not expected to furnish such material as part of his or her duties (as is the case with compliance officers) and gives information that ultimately leads to a penalty being imposed on an insider dealer. In the years from its inception to 2003, the SEC's whistle-blower programme paid out more than $107 million to 33 whistle-blowers, providing huge incentives for individuals to report misconduct to the authorities. The idea of adopting such a policy in the UK was considered during the early-1990s, but rejected as 'too American'. (Interestingly, the Market Abuse Regulation of 2016 have expressly supported the use of financial incentives for this purpose). Nevertheless, the FSA/FCA has done its best to encourage the emergence of a whistle-blowing culture.[1] Rightly or wrongly, it has been claimed that one major criminal investigation for insider dealing in recent years began with a tip-off to the authorities from the suspect's (former) wife's lover.[2]

Those with relevant information to report can email whistle@fca.org.uk), call 0207 066 9200 (a special market abuse hotline, originally established by the FSA and now supervised by the FCA), or write to the FCA Intelligence Department at 25 The North Colonnade, London E14 5HS). Callers are not required to give their identity or contact details, but are encouraged to provide the names of those involved in the alleged misconduct, key dates, the *modus operandi* of the wrongdoing, and the availability of any supporting documents or evidence. Paragraph 74 of the MAR 2016 stipulates that regulators and firms must have in place specific procedures for whistle-blowing and provisions to 'protect [whistle-blowers] from retaliation'. Of course, not all whistle-blowers are the same; they range from extremely honest people who are genuinely worried about their careers to those whose motives are more mixed, sometimes being laced with spite, jealousy, or a desire to deflect attention from themselves.

Observant brokers in the finance industry detect considerably more cases (than whistle-blowers) as part of their work. Sometimes, they are fairly obvious. For example, in 2015 an individual contacted his broker to ask whether it was possible to reverse a trade he had made the previous day, as he thought that it might have constituted insider dealing: 'I fear I may have been guilty or be judged to be guilty of insider trading'. The broker declined to do this and reported the trade to the FCA as suspicious.[3] At other times, the trade simply appears 'out of character' with the client and his previous investment history, such as the sudden purchase of high risk options by someone who has only previously dealt in stable 'blue chip' shares. In a case that came to court in 2016, it was reportedly alleged that a business analyst, called his neighbour in the early evening of 28th May 2012 as the

---

1   Michael Filby, 'The Enforcement of Insider Dealing under the Financial Services and Markets Act 2000', 2003, p.334.

2   *Daily Telegraph*, 26 February 2009.

3   FCA Press Release, 13 May 2016; FCA Final Notice, No MST00007, 5 May 2016.

board was meeting to discuss the announcement of a deal. The following morning, the neighbour called his broker and bought £20,000 of shares in the company concerned and, unusually for his portfolio, £4,000 worth of options, saying he had a 'hunch' about a possible takeover. The public announcement of a takeover followed three days later. This combination of events prompted a warning of possible illegal trading from the relevant broker to his employer. In turn, the employer duly filed a suspicious transaction report (see below) the following day, triggering an FCA probe and prosecution.[4] Under the Market Abuse Regulation (MAR) 2016, firms are required to ensure that their staff are trained to identify behaviour, orders, and transactions which could constitute actual or attempted insider dealing.

Complex Event Processing (CEP)

In the modern era one of the most common means by which insider-dealing is detected can be found in the increasingly sophisticated electronic surveillance systems that are available to monitor sales volume and price movements in publicly traded shares in the financial services industry. Such 'complex event processing' (CEP) technology will generate an automatic alert on any movement that exceeds certain parameters, and an investigator can then see whether it precedes an unusual announcement by the relevant company. Since the advent of the MAR 2016, firms are required to have systems capable of analysing every transaction and order they make, individually and comparatively, to a technical standard proportionate to the scale, size and nature of their business. If they appear suspicious, finance industry firms must report these electronically identified movements to the FCA's market-monitoring department.

Nevertheless, it is not a new phenomenon. In early 2000, an Inland Revenue officer in the capital gains tax clearance section in Solihull, which advised companies considering mergers or takeovers, admitted insider dealing some two years earlier using information gleaned from his workplace. Although the profits were comparatively modest, the trades appear to have been picked up by the LSE's Imas market-surveillance computer. The exchange then

---

4   *Financial Times*, 29 November 2016.

alerted the DTI, which launched a criminal investigation.[5]

Reporting Suspicious Transactions

Firms and individuals who were professionally engaged in the arrangement or execution of transactions were first required to notify the relevant authorities (then the FSA now the FCA) of suspicious transactions by Article 6(9) of the EU's Market Abuse Directive (MAD) 2003, which required that they act without delay where they had 'reasonable grounds' to suspect that a transaction might constitute market abuse (including insider dealing), whether committed by their own employees, their clients, or counter-parties. Until recently, they did this by providing suspicious transaction reports (STRs) to the regulator. However, the MAR 2016, which replaced most of MAD, extended the disclosure obligation on firms and trading venues to include reporting suspicious 'orders' (which include quotes and requests for quotes) as attempted market abuse (now prohibited by Article 14(a) MAR), in addition to actual transactions. As a result, these reports are now called 'suspicious transaction and order reports' (STORs).

Firms and trading venues with questions about how to complete or submit a report can call the FCA's STOR helpline. Such reports are commonplace, with most firms operating on the basis that, if there is any doubt, it is prudent to report a transaction. There were 336 STRs in the seven months from July 2005 (when the system began) to February 2006.[6] In the five years between July 2005 and June 2010 there were 1,485 of them.[7] The number has since increased further. In late-2013 the FCA said it had received more than 1,000 STRs over the previous 12-month period, compared with 739 the year before that. There were 1,626 submitted in the year to April 2014, and 1,831 cases over the following 12 months.[8]

This growth is probably not due to increased abuse. Much more likely, it is an indication of a greater general awareness of what constitutes insider

---

5   *The Guardian*, 7 April 2000.

6   Margaret Cole, 'Insider Dealing in the City'. Talk at the London School of Economics, delivered on 17 March 2007.

7   Paul Barnes, 'Insider Dealing and Market Abuse: The UK's Record on Enforcement', 2011, pp.174–189.

8   *Daily Telegraph*, 12 July 2016.

trading, its consequences, and the need to report it. Most STRS/STORs (up to 95 per cent of them) relate to potential cases of insider dealing, particularly in equity markets.[9] For example, of the 1,831 cases in the year to April 2015, 1,604 were linked to suspicions about the misuse of information (i.e. insider dealing), while just 214 related to suspected market manipulation.[10] (These STRs were reported to be of a generally high quality and quite properly filed).[11] Similarly, from 3rd July to 31st December 2016 the FCA received 1,526 STORs relating to insider dealing and just 372 with regard to market manipulation. The vast majority of the former related to equities (rather than fixed income, commodity, or foreign exchange assets).[12]

A failure by those in the finance industry to alert the FCA to a suspicious transaction can lead to a significant civil penalty. In 2009, a trading desk manager at a retail stock-broking firm was fined £20,000 after failing to identify a transaction that was being conducted on the basis of inside information, despite clear warning signs to that effect. As a result, his firm was used to facilitate a transaction made on the basis of inside information. In mitigation, the FSA noted that the manager in question had reliably reported suspicious trades on earlier occasions, suggesting a purely momentary aberration or loss of focus on his part.[13]

The regulator can penalise a firm merely for having unsatisfactory systems for preventing and detecting market abuse and producing STORs. In 2016, the FCA found a company's systems failed to ensure it had proper controls in place in this respect. In part (there were many other aspects to the decision) this was because they relied on employees making personal judgments as to whether a transaction was sufficiently suspicious to require escalation to their compliance department. This was particularly important because the company's business activities meant that it regularly (and quite properly) received inside information, and so required a robust system of controls. The company was fined £1.2 million pursuant to section 206

---

9   FCA Final Notice to W H Ireland Limited, Ref No 140773, 22 February 2016.

10   *Daily Telegraph*, 12 July 2016.

11   *Fair and Effective Markets Review: Final Report*, 2015, London, p.91.

12   FCA Press Release, 28 February 2017.

13   FSA Final Notice, Ref No. MXL01331, 1 September 2009.

FSMA and restricted for a period of 72 days from taking on new clients in its corporate broking division, even though there had, apparently, been no instances of market abuse actually going undetected by the firm. (The regulator also recognised that the firm had co-operated with its investigation and was actively addressing these problems).[14]

FCA Monitoring

In addition to relying on STORs and whistle-blowers the FCA also conducts its own electronic market surveillance to bring cases to light. Until late-2011 this was done by the Surveillance and Automated Business Reporting Engine (SABRE) II programme, which provided automatic alerts of transactions that might be examples of insider dealing. This was replaced by the similar, but considerably enhanced, ZEN system, provided with raw data from the financial companies that the FCA regulates via millions of transaction reports each day (poor reporting can lead to heavy fines). A new Market Data Processor (MDP) was due to replace ZEN in 2017. Under the supervision of Patrick Spens, Head of Market Monitoring at the FCA from 2009 to 2016, the regulator's market monitoring team was considerably expanded, with extra quantitative analysts being recruited. Such analysts write algorithms that can identify unusual trading patterns and so potential cases of market abuse; some of these have already secured criminal prosecutions for insider dealing.[15]

Of course, it is not a precise science, and often requires difficult judgments to be made. By way of example, in 2013 the FSA dropped an investigation into a hedge fund that arose from a review of what it mistakenly thought looked like abnormal trading activity. It transpired that the significance of very small (but vital) periods of time to what was an entirely legitimate 'short' sale was missed.[16]

The regulator's markets' experts also focus on sudden spikes in trading levels that appear inherently suspicious. More specifically, it seems that the

---

14   FCA Press Release, 23 February 2016; FCA Final Notice to W H Ireland Limited, 22 February 2016.

15   *Financial Times*, 2 July 2015.

16   *Wall Street Journal*, 4 January 2014.

activities of already identified 'persons of interest', dealers who have regularly featured in STR/STORs in the past, and who trade in high volumes close to the publication of important announcements, are subject to special scrutiny.[17]

Investigating Insider Dealing

Once a suspicious transaction, that suggests possible insider dealing, has come to the attention of the FCA, its Enforcement and Market Oversight Division (EMOD) will make a decision on whether to investigate the matter further. On one analysis, between April 2013 and September 2016 the FCA opened 65 criminal investigations specific to insider dealing, of which 54 cases were still open on the latter date.[18] According to another, based on data obtained through a freedom of information request by *Bloomberg News*, it started 70 insider-dealing investigations in 2016 alone, more than double any other year in the last decade, with many more being commenced in early-2017.[19] However, most reported cases do not get that far. Although individuals and their transactions may initially have been flagged up as 'suspicious', action is often not taken after initial scrutiny. The great majority of the STRs filed between 2005 and 2010 did not trigger a formal investigation.[20]

In 2017, Jamie Symington, Director of Investigations at the FCA, noted that the regulator would not necessarily investigate every case that technically justified such action that fell within its remit (not just those involving insider dealing): 'The powers and resources that we have to investigate need to be deployed most efficiently and effectively in delivering on our objectives in the public interest'. However, where the suspected misconduct was considered serious and the potential harm significant the FCA would expect to open an investigation, the decision to do so being taken jointly by

---

17   David Kirk, 'Enforcement of Criminal Sanctions for Market Abuse: Practicalities, Problem Solving and Pitfalls', 2016, p.317.

18   *Money Marketing*, 23 September 2016.

19   Bloomberg, 20 April 2017.

20   Paul Barnes, 'Insider Dealing and Market Abuse: The UK's Record on Enforcement', 2011, pp.174–189.

senior staff from the Enforcement and Supervision Divisions.[21]Where they do lead to an investigation, most of those who are subject to FCA scrutiny will initially be unaware that their trading patterns are being examined. The FCA might (or might not) alert their employer, if they work for a finance industry company, but would not usually want the firm to embark on its own investigation (whether an internal audit report or external report), as it might prejudice its own on-going monitoring of the suspect by alerting him or her to exposure.[22] Even when launched, many FSA/FCA investigations do not progress far and are abandoned fairly swiftly. The FCA can also issue a private warning at any stage in the procedure to formally close an investigation.

The FCA's Criminal Prosecution Team, a special part of the Enforcement and Market Oversight Division (formerly the EFCD), plays an important role in advising on the investigation process and whether a prosecution should be brought. It also takes the lead role in litigating criminal cases. More specifically, it advises investigators about searches under warrant, interviews, evidential sufficiency, disclosure, and confiscation work. Its ranks include senior barristers seconded from private practice as well as its own internal lawyers, one of whom is appointed as the FCA's Chief Criminal Counsel. Perhaps significantly for the regulator's future direction when it comes to enforcement, in 2017, Vincent Coughlin QC, an enormously experienced barrister who had had considerable exposure to white-collar crime during his professional career, was appointed to the position. The EMOD also contains an Evidence Processing Unit, which includes, *inter alia*, specialist digital forensic and electronic discovery teams, to assist the regulator in investigations and help with a wide range of evidential processing tasks.

The Investigative Interview

The investigative interview with a suspect can be a crucial part both of criminal prosecutions and regulatory actions for insider dealing. Given the large overlap between the two, both are usually possibilities when suspected

---

21   Speech by Jamie Symington, Director of Investigations at the FCA, at the Legal Week Banking Litigation and Regulation Forum, London, 15 June 2017.

22   FCA, *The Enforcement Guide* 01/04/2014, para 3.23.

instances of such dealing first come to light. As a result, FCA investigative interviews will nearly always aim to satisfy the higher standard required of criminal actions, even if this course is not ultimately pursued, and so will be: '... subject to all the safeguards of the relevant Police and Criminal Evidence Act Codes'.[23] For example and typically, the FCA noted that the family friend mentioned in relation to the case of *R v Ryan Willmott* (see *Chapter 1*), who was eventually dealt with under the regulatory regime, had: '... his first interview under caution in accordance with the Police and Criminal Evidence Act 1984 which took place at an early stage in the Authority's insider dealing investigation'.[24]

Taking such precautions preserves the admissibility at trial of any resulting 'confession', which is defined under section 82(1) Police and Criminal Evidence Act (PACE) 1984 as a statement that is 'wholly or partly adverse' to its maker, *if* the criminal route is eventually adopted. Under section 67(9) of PACE, anyone charged with the conduct of a criminal investigation must follow the safeguards contained in the Statute and its attendant Codes of Practice when conducting investigations into criminal offences. This includes, for example, officers of the Serious Fraud Office.[25] More pertinently, it also extends to officers of the FCA who are investigating cases of insider dealing.

There are two ways in which someone can be formally interviewed in a criminal investigation. They may be cautioned and questioned after attending for interview voluntarily, usually by appointment. In these circumstances, the FCA officer administering the caution must first tell the suspect that he or she is free to leave at any time. Such interviews will normally be carried out at the FCA Head Office in London and there is no requirement for the police to be present or involved. Alternatively, an FCA officer who has reasonable grounds to suspect someone of committing an offence may ask the police to make an arrest in order to question them, whether after meeting them by appointment or (much more commonly) by detaining

---

23   FCA, *The Enforcement Guide* 01/04/2014, para 4.21.

24   FCA Final Notice, 30 March 2015.

25   *R v Director of the Serious Fraud Office, ex p. Saunders* [1988] Crim LR 837.

them at their home or place of work.[26]

FSA/FCA officers themselves have no powers of arrest beyond those of any ordinary member of the public. However, in August 2005 the FSA signed a memorandum of understanding with the Association of Chief Police Officers (ACPO), replacing an earlier agreement from 2003, to record best practice for co-operation between the police and the regulator. This is still in force with regard to the FCA, and sets out an agreed practice in the event that a suspect has to be arrested or the regulator seeks the execution of a search warrant.

This course might be adopted where it appears that inviting an individual to attend for interview voluntarily could prejudice an ongoing investigation and risk the destruction of evidence, the dissipation of assets, or even the escape of the suspect. It might also be done where a suspect declines to attend a voluntary interview. Where an arrest has been carried out, any ensuing interview will usually be conducted at a police station, whether in The Square Mile or local to the suspect if they are detained outside central London. An arrest will usually (but not invariably) be followed by an immediate interview. Under paragraph 9.2 of the Memorandum of Understanding of 2005, a police representative can be present during the interview to provide technical assistance and guidance with regard to compliance with the Codes of Practice under PACE, although this is not necessary (and often not done); questioning will be carried out by FCA officers.

A suspect might be charged at the conclusion of the initial interview. Frequently, however, he or she will be released (on police bail if necessary) so that a further interview, or even series of interviews, can be held in the light of the initial questioning or (more commonly) after seized documents (whether electronic or paper) have been examined and their contents properly digested, or other enquiries made. This can be a lengthy process, meaning that formal action might take place long after the initial arrest. For example, in one case (mentioned in *Chapter 7* of this book) the suspect was first arrested three years before he was eventually charged with insider dealing in late-2016, albeit that this was an extreme case.

---

26   Sarah Clarke, *Insider Dealing: Law and Practice*, 2013, p.246.

More typically can be considered the abortive FSA investigation into a (legitimate) hedge fund in 2013 (dealt with elsewhere). A portfolio manager, was summoned to a crack-of-dawn meeting at his employer's corporate headquarters, where he was met by the company's compliance chief, who informed him that police and FSA officers were there to arrest him for insider trading. At the same time as he was being arrested, police and FSA officials arrived at his home, which they searched before seizing several phones and computers. Searches were also being conducted at the homes of two founding partners of the hedge fund, who were also arrested. Officers also raided offices, seizing computers and documents. The three men were brought to a police station in central London. Once there, FSA officials informed them (separately) that the portfolio manager was suspected of leaking inside information and that the two founding partners were suspected of basing a short sale of stock on that information. On this occasion, and slightly unusually, the men were not questioned immediately. The (newly established) FCA's interviews with the suspects were initially scheduled for May 2013. However, it subsequently delayed them until mid-September. On December 6, the FCA issued a short statement saying that the three men were 'no longer under investigation'.[27] No one was ever charged with any offence.

Section 58 and Code C of PACE provide that suspects in criminal cases must have access to legal advice if they desire it. In insider dealing cases they would usually be well-advised to insist on specialist legal representation, rather than on a general practice solicitor, because of the fairly arcane nature of the subject and because their lawyer might, if appropriate, help steer the FCA towards a regulatory rather than a criminal action (an option not normally seen in other parts of the criminal justice system). Ideally, those instructed in insider dealing cases will understand how a trade fits into a client's wider investment strategy, rather than simply mastering the relevant email trail.[28] Suspects must also be cautioned before being questioned, by dint of paragraph 10.1 of Code C of PACE, while under Code E their interviews must be properly tape-recorded. There are numerous other

---

27   *Wall Street Journal,* 4 January 2014.

28   Sarah Wallace and Samantha Leung, 'Leave No Stone Unturned', *New Law Journal,* 16 June 2017, p.11.

provisions regulating the circumstances in which suspects are interviewed, such as the provision of rest breaks and refreshment.

As with other criminal offences, a failure to follow 'significant and substantial' (rather than minor) provisions in the relevant codes to PACE and the Statute itself, when investigating insider dealing, can lead to any statements that are adverse to the maker that were elicited by the questioning being excluded from an ensuing criminal trial under section 78(1) of PACE, on the basis that their being adduced would have such an adverse effect on the fairness of proceedings that the court ought not to admit them: *R v Walsh* (1989) 91 Cr App R 161. It might also make it easier for defence counsel to argue that the statement had been obtained by oppression or (more pertinently) in consequence of anything said or done which was likely in the circumstances at the time to render it unreliable, leading to exclusion under section 76(2) of PACE.

The privilege against self-incrimination means that a suspect has the right not to answer the questions put to him or her (the so-called 'right to silence') when interviewed under caution by FCA investigators, just as he or she does when questioned directly by the police. As Jamie Symington, the Director of Investigations at the FCA, noted in June 2017: 'No doubt some subjects of those sorts of investigations will stand on their right to silence etc. They are entitled to do so, and we respect that'.[29]

However, as with other crimes, it is not an unqualified right. A failure by a defendant who has been cautioned and allowed access to legal advice (if desired) to mention any fact that, in the circumstances existing at the time, he or she could reasonably have been expected to mention, and which he or she later relies on in his or her defence, may be the subject of adverse judicial comment, allowing the tribunal to draw appropriate adverse inferences, under section 34 of the Criminal Justice and Public Order Act 1994.

Such inferences are not drawn lightly: *R v Argent* [1997] 2 Cr. App. R. 27. Very importantly, at least for insider dealing allegations, in *R v Roble* [1997] EWCA Crim 118, Lord Justice Rose stated that a good reason not to draw an adverse inference might well arise if the: '... nature of the offence, or the

---

material in the hands of the police is so complex, or relates to matters so long ago, that no sensible immediate response is feasible'. Someone accused of numerous historic cases of insider dealing, dating back over a considerable period of time, might well feel that they should not attempt to explain how they came to trade in particular securities, especially shortly after arrest. Perhaps for this reason, *inter alia*, it seems that despite the risks of an adverse inference direction, several of those being interviewed for insider dealing in recent years have decided not to answer questions, after receiving legal advice. For example, in 2000, a former LSE employee may have declined to be interviewed by Department of Trade and Industry (DTI) officials.[30] Similarly, it appears that a hedge fund trader may have initially refused to answer questions in 2014 when questioned by the FCA.[31] From a potential 'defence' point of view, any response, if it *is* made in these circumstances, should usually be measured, pointing out the potential difficulties of tracing/recollecting long past events.

The Decision to Prosecute

The advent of civil penalties under FSMA 2000 raised difficult questions about the relationship between the two regimes, civil and criminal, not least because of the very significant legal overlap between the conduct proscribed. These have never been settled in an entirely satisfactory manner, perhaps unsurprisingly, given that the relevant provisions in Part V of the CJA 1993 were originally drafted as a 'stand alone' regime for combating insider dealing and not in anticipation of the responsibility being shared (some would say diluted) by the introduction of the civil regime.

Of course, occasionally a suspect might be liable under the regulatory regime without satisfying the requirements of its criminal counterpart. Although there is a substantial overlap between the two regimes, it is not total. For example, section 118B(e) FSMA (now replaced by MAR) provided that an insider was someone who had inside information which he knew *'or could reasonably be expected to know'* was inside information. The latter (italicised) addition is not contained in the 1993 Act, which simply requires

---

30 *Daily Telegraph*, 12 December 2000.

31 *Bloomberg*, 19 March 2015.

knowledge. Even so, in most cases both options are potentially open to the regulator even if the standard of proof will always be different should matters reach a court hearing: beyond reasonable doubt in a criminal case and on a balance of probabilities in a civil one: see further and especially, *Chapter 3*.

According to Alistair Darling MP, then (2000) the Chief Secretary to the Treasury, the new civil sanctions would 'complement, not replace, the existing criminal offence'. This requires a rationale for distinguishing between the two forms of action. It is at least arguable that there should be a hierarchy of gravity; with moral culpability being decisive in deciding which route is selected by the FCA. Less serious matters would be dealt with via the civil process and more heinous cases prosecuted. However, this issue is complicated by the absence of any requirement of dishonesty in the *mens rea* for the criminal offence (see *Chapter 4*). Even so, in March 1999 Howard Davies, the FSA's first chief executive, declared to the Parliamentary Joint Committee on Financial Services and Markets that: 'We would not see the civil route as a cheap alternative to the criminal route. We think that if there is criminal intent then the criminal route should be chosen and that is what you should attempt to do'. This suggestion has not always been followed in practice.

As has been noted, the FCA's decision-making on what insider (and other market abuse) cases to prosecute, within a finite budget, is partly guided by what will be 'best value for money'.[32] The gravity of the offence, and the ease or difficulty of proving it, inevitably enter into this equation. A very egregious case of insider dealing, which is readily provable, will almost certainly be indicted. A minor case, which will be very expensive to establish in a forensic environment, might well not be.

In July 2000, in response to a question from Howard Flight MP, Melanie Johnson MP, then Economic Secretary to the Treasury, observed that the FSA (now the FCA) would determine at the beginning of any investigation which route (criminal or civil) was most appropriate.[33] However, this is not always clear at a very early stage in such an investigation. As a result,

---

32 Aleksandra Jordanoska, 'Case Management in Complex Fraud Trials: Actors and Strategies in Achieving Procedural Efficiency', 2017, p.347.

33 Seventh Standing Committee on Delegated Legislation, 13 July 2000.

deciding whether the criminal or market abuse route should be adopted is sometimes not taken until the investigation is at a relatively advanced stage.[34] Even so, once a suspect is aware that he is being investigated — for example, after he or she is arrested and interviewed — a choice as to forum often has to be made fairly swiftly.

Of course, this vital decision is not unique to the UK. It is found in many other jurisdictions with a bifurcated system of penalties. In Hong Kong, for example, a similar dual regime means that the Securities and Futures Commission there can refer a suspected insider dealing case either to the Financial Secretary to consider the institution of civil proceedings before the Market Misconduct Tribunal or, alternatively, can send it to the Department of Justice to consider the institution of criminal prosecutions.[35]

When deciding whether or not to bring a criminal action, the FCA applies the Code for Crown Prosecutors. This is a public document, issued by the Director of Public Prosecutions (DPP), setting out the general principles Crown prosecutors should follow in all criminal cases, not just those brought by the CPS. The Health and Safety Executive, and all other designated prosecuting bodies, also employ the code. Under it, the decision to prosecute is based on a two-stage test. A senior FCA internal lawyer or experienced counsel in private practice who has been instructed by the Enforcement and Market Oversight Division (formerly EFCD)'s Legal Department will normally advise on whether it has been met, although the final decision on this issue is taken by the FCA's senior officers.

The Two-Stage Test

Firstly, the test requires that the FCA must anticipate a 'realistic prospect' of securing a conviction on each count brought against every defendant indicted.[36] The most important factor when making this decision is, inevitably, an assessment of the legally admissible evidence available against the accused person and the FCA's likely ability to satisfy the high criminal standard of proof, as well as their willingness (where relevant) to commit the

---

34   Clare Montgomery *et al*, *Fraud: Criminal Law and Procedure*, 2015, at D.5.06.

35   Rita Cheung, 'Criminal Prosecution for Insider Dealing: a Hong Kong Perspective', 2010, p.163.

36   Iwona Seredyńska, *Insider Dealing and Criminal Law: Dangerous Liaisons*, 2012, pp.131–132.

substantial resources often required for success in the criminal arena. As the Treasury Committee noted in 1999, when the FSMA was passing through Parliament: '... although the FSA's new civil powers will be useful, we believe that criminal prosecutions should be set in train whenever the evidence is strong enough'.[37] In reality, this comment does not quite stand up to analysis, as other factors, such as culpability, are also considered (see below).

If the evidential part of the test cannot be met, a criminal prosecution will not be brought. For example, during the 2004 trial of someone accused of being a member of an insider ring (three of whom had already pleaded guilty), lawyers for the Serious Fraud Office (the prosecuting authority in this case) told the court that the conspiracy was not just limited to four people. Secretly taped conversations implicated others, but there was not enough admissible evidence to prosecute them. As prosecuting counsel Timothy Langdale QC observed to the jury: 'You will hear that, plainly, there were others involved ... I cannot provide the evidence about quite how they [the others] got the [inside] information'.[38]

Where there is not sufficient evidence for a prosecution, the civil process, employing a lesser standard of proof, not following the stricter criminal rules of evidence, or requiring the use of a jury, and providing for a swifter general procedure, one that also allows the FCA to 'settle' cases on terms, has many attractions.[39] Unfortunately, issues of evidential sufficiency are not always easy to determine, especially very early in an investigation.

The second limb in the prosecution test stipulates that even if there is enough admissible evidence, criminal action must also be deemed to be in the 'public interest'. As a result, the FCA considers factors other than the available evidence when making its decision. Some observers have even suggested that these are often more important than evidential considerations, although this is open to question.[40] Many of these factors are set out in the FCA's *Enforcement Guide*. Amongst them are:

---

37   Jonathan Fisher, *Fighting Fraud and Financial Crime*, 2010, p.10.

38   *The Guardian*, 5 June 2004; *The Guardian*, 7 January 2004.

39   Margaret Cole, 'Insider Dealing in the City'. Talk at the London School of Economics, delivered on 17 March 2007.

40   Clare Montgomery *et al*, *Fraud: Criminal Law and Procedure*, 2015, at D.5.06.

- the likely gravity of any sentence that would be imposed after a conviction (a significant sentence would encourage prosecution);
- whether there were any identifiable victims who had directly suffered a loss (rare in insider dealing cases);
- the effect that criminal proceedings will have on redress for any victims, although potential defendants will not avoid prosecution simply because they are able to pay compensation;
- the effect of the misconduct on market confidence; the scale of the profits made or losses avoided as a consequence of the dealing and the frequency with which it occurred;
- whether there are grounds for believing that the misconduct is likely to be repeated; the value of a deterrent example (where appropriate);
- any previous convictions or disciplinary findings against the accused person; the degree of the suspect's dishonesty and abuse of trust;
- the culpability of specific individuals when there has been a group enterprise (Were they a ringleader?);
- the personal circumstances of the suspect and their willingness to co-operate with the FCA (especially assisting in the investigation and prosecution of someone else).

The importance attached by the FCA to these factors will vary from case to case.[41]

More generally, the FCA must, so far as it is reasonably possible, act in a way that is compatible with its strategic objective of ensuring that markets function well, and its operational objective of enhancing the integrity of the UK financial system. At the same time the regulator and its enforcement team is also mindful of the potential cost of such actions and that insider trials take up a large amount of court time, and are correspondingly expensive for the Court Service.[42] In *practice*, such policy factors appear to mean that relatively amateurish, small or unsuccessful cases of insider trading, where there are special mitigating circumstances, and swift co-operation

---

41   FCA *The Enforcement Guide*, 01/04/2014, para 12.8–12.9.

42   David Kirk, 'Enforcement of Criminal Sanctions for Market Abuse: Practicalities, Problem Solving and Pitfalls', 2016, p.320.

by the suspect, can be dealt with via the civil regime.

Two cases from 2016 illustrate some of the factors that might support adopting a regulatory approach. Both involved comparatively modest sums, opportunistic (rather than carefully planned) and 'one off' (rather than sustained) behaviour, swift remorse and regret, a relative lack of sophistication, and quick, candid, and very full assistance to the FCA. However, it should be stressed that in both cases the regulator's Final Notice made no mention at all of even the possibility of prosecution under the 1993 Act, and it may well be that some of the essential prerequisites for such an action were absent, and that no criminal offence (rather than civil wrong) had been committed (even technically), making regulatory action the only option open to the FCA.

In September 2014, a shareholder attempted to sell his entire holding in a PLC, of which he was a board member, after being made an insider in relation to a proposed share placing by the company that was intended to raise £3.5 million at a substantial discount to its then prevailing share price (which would drive the latter down). He successfully disposed of 10,000 shares, avoiding a loss of just £1,900. Furthermore, he disclosed the inside information to another shareholder who (unlike him) was unaware of it, albeit that this individual took no action as a result.[43] The individual was subsequently dealt with under the regulatory procedure, censured, and fined £59,557 for market abuse. The authority noted his extensive co-operation during its investigation. He had voluntarily travelled to the UK from abroad to attend an interview under caution, where he had quickly made admissions that greatly reduced the time and cost of the investigation. He then freely provided additional documents to the authority. He also swiftly offered to provide restitution to those who had purchased his 10,000 shares.[44]

In 2016, the FCA fined a financial adviser £36,285 and banned him from dealing for two years (under section 56 FSMA) for insider dealing. The adviser had purchased shares in a PLC for £15,000, using inside information accidentally provided to him by his employer, despite being warned not to do so. After the information was made public he sold his shares, making

---

43   FCA Final Notice, 15 July 2016.

44   Ibid.

a profit of just £3,498. The following day he thought better of the transaction and contacted his broker to ask whether it was possible to reverse the trade, as he feared that he might have been guilty of insider dealing. The broker declined to do this and (unsurprisingly given the 'anxious' man's candour) reported the trade to the FCA using an STR. The man wishing to reverse the transaction, who was experiencing acute financial hardship at the time, made full admissions to the FCA at a very early stage of their investigation and swiftly agreed to settle the matter.[45] (His early admissions in an interview under caution and financial problems also reduced the regulatory penalty imposed).[46]

Much more serious cases of insider dealing, where a prosecution clearly *might* at least have been considered by the FSA (now FCA), have also sometimes been dealt with via the regulatory route, where there was quite *exceptional* mitigation, such as (in particular) dealers actively bringing their own behaviour to the regulator's notice. For example, in 2008 an executive chairman of an AIM listed company asked a friend to buy shares in the same company on his behalf, having become aware of a forthcoming takeover announcement. After it was duly made public the two men made over £40,000 selling the shares. There were aggravating features in the case, not least the executive chairman's breach of trust. In its Final Notice, the FSA hinted that in other circumstances a prosecution might have been appropriate ('the FSA may have brought criminal proceedings against [the man]'). Even so, the executive chairman (like his friend) was merely dealt with under section 118(2) FSMA (now replaced by MAR), albeit that he received a very substantial penalty payment in addition to being ordered to make a much more modest disgorgement of profits. The reason for this apparently benign approach, expressly noted in his Final Notice, seems to have been the quite exceptional level of co-operation. Most importantly, and very unusually, '[The man] approached the FSA', and appears to have drawn the matter to their attention.[47] If he had not done so, the case may

45 *Financial Times*, 13 May 2016.

46 FCA Final Notice, Ref. No. MST00007, 5 May 2016.

47 Sarah Clarke, *Insider Dealing: Law and Practice*, 2013, pp.251–252. *The Guardian*, 3 November 2008. FSA Final Notice, 12 November 2008.

never have come to light at all.

Two years later, the CEO of a Turkish energy company, was also dealt with via the regulatory route for a very similar reason, after making a £267,000 profit on the purchase and sale of oil shares based on insider knowledge of exploratory drilling tests. Again, the FSA noted his very high degree of co-operation: '… [Y]ou approached the FSA and made admissions as to your conduct'. It seems that when he initially traded the CEO (a foreign national) had not realised that what he was doing was prohibited. His solicitors had subsequently contacted the FSA at his behest, informing them as to what had occurred and providing full details of his share transactions. The CEO then came to London to attend a voluntary interview at the FSA's offices. Without this openness, the regulator noted that the: 'FSA may have brought criminal proceedings against you'.[48]

An inherent problem in these situations is that a suspect might be highly co-operative, and make swift admissions, in the hope that this will encourage the FCA to have recourse to the regulatory rather than the criminal route, only to find them being used against him as a confession if the regulator decides to bring a criminal prosecution. (Normally, the only decision in a criminal case is whether to prosecute or not; there is no 'lesser' option). Closely connected to this problem, and rather unusually, a suspect in such cases is able to actively influence the route followed by the FCA (civil or criminal) by making representations about which forum is most suitable (usually through his solicitor) during the early stages of the investigation.

Of course, if the FCA were foolish enough to suggest that making admissions would make it more likely that the regulatory route would be taken, any ensuing confession would almost certainly be excluded under section 76(2)(b) PACE for unreliability, because it had been obtained by an inducement: *R v Fulling* [1987] 2 All ER 65. It might also be excluded under section 78 PACE for general unfairness. Instead, the possibility of the more lenient route being adopted hangs in the air, and is something to be gauged and initiated by the suspect's legal representative in discussions with the FCA.

It can be a delicate and difficult issue. In an analogous situation, in 2017,

---

48   FSA Final Notice, 12 February 2010; *Daily Telegraph*, 16 February 2010.

one convicted defendant applied to the Criminal Cases Review Commission (CCRC), asking that his conviction for rigging the Libor interest rate, for which he had received eleven years imprisonment, be referred to the Court of Appeal. Early on in the investigative process he had made admissions to the SFO as part of a SOCPA interview (see *Chapter 6*) and agreed to co-operate with the agency. However, he subsequently pleaded 'not guilty' and was convicted at trial, his earlier admissions being used against him: *R v Hayes* [2015] EWCA Crim 1944. When he approached the CCRC it was, in part, on the basis that he had made them not because they were true but because he was afraid that otherwise he would be extradited to America where he was wanted for similar charges.[49]

Although enormously important, the decision to have recourse to the criminal rather than civil route is not normally susceptible to judicial review. In *R v McQuoid* [2009] EWCA Crim 1301 Lord Judge noted, in the Court of Appeal, that it could not be suggested that the previous policy of using the regulatory system misled the appellant into thinking that insider dealing: '… if proved, would be, or could be, other than criminal, or that he had some kind of reasonable expectation that it would or even that it might'. Even so, criminal prosecutions are not embarked upon lightly.

For the first seven years after section 52 CJA 1993 came into force, section 61(2) of the same Statute required that they receive the consent of the Secretary of State or the DPP. This is no longer the case. In *Regina (Uberoi and Another) v City of Westminster Magistrates' Court* [2009] 1 WLR 1905, the prospective defendants in an insider dealing case challenged the power of the FSA to bring a prosecution without the consent of these officers. The Queen's Bench Divisional Court, Lord Justice May presiding, decided that, in the light of section 402 FSMA 2000, it was no longer necessary in prosecutions brought by the regulator.

FCA prosecutions still need high-level internal authorisation. For example, a decision to commence criminal proceedings normally has to be made by the RDC chairman or, in an urgent case (and if the chairman is not available) by an RDC deputy chairman. In an exceptionally urgent case, such as

---

49   *The Guardian*, 31 January 2017.

one where it is necessary to protect the interests of consumers, the matter might be decided by the Director of Enforcement or, in his or her absence, another member of the FCA's executive of at least director of division level.[50] Sarah Clarke (a former senior FSA/FCA lawyer) notes that the relevant officer will usually have been provided with a draft indictment and other information. He or she will also normally meet with the case team before making that decision.[51] If they decide to prosecute, the FCA has no power to charge a suspect in its own right. The police will do this on their behalf.

Consequences of the Decision as to Forum

The decision as to which route to adopt has enormous consequences in the UK. Early on, the FSA appears to have decided not to risk breaching 'double jeopardy' rules by pursuing both criminal and regulatory sanctions in the same case. It is still the FCA's policy not to commence a criminal prosecution for market misconduct where it has brought — or is seeking to bring — disciplinary proceedings for market abuse that arise from substantially the same allegations.[52] Conversely, if a criminal prosecution is brought but an acquittal ensues, and despite the difference in the standard of proof: 'It is the FCA's policy not to impose a sanction for market abuse where a person is being prosecuted for market misconduct or has been finally convicted or acquitted of market misconduct (following the exhaustion of all appeal processes) in a criminal prosecution arising from substantially the same allegations'.[53]

This means that acquitted defendants will usually keep the proceeds of alleged (but rejected by a jury) cases of insider dealing, without facing any form of civil process.[54] For example, it appears that in 2012 two acquitted defendants retained the almost £600,000 profits made from their trading after they were found 'not guilty'. One of them had handed over one million Euros (£806,000) to the court, prior to the criminal trial resulting in a

---

50   FCA *The Enforcement Guide* 01/04/2014, para 12.4A.

51   Sarah Clarke, *Insider Dealing: Law and Practice*, 2013, p.258.

52   FCA *The Enforcement Guide* 01/04/2014, para 12.10.

53   Ibid, para 12.10.

54   Michael Filby, 'The Enforcement of Insider Dealing under the Financial Services and Markets Act 2000', 2003, p.341.

verdict of not guilty, which could have been seized if she had been convicted. After acquittal, prosecutors were given 24-hours to raise any objections to the money being returned but do not appear to have done so. The other accused had not paid any of the (very much smaller amount of) money that they made into court, but after being found 'not guilty' could not have been subject to confiscation proceedings.[55]

It should be noted that such an approach is analogous to, and matched by, the courts' interpretation of Part 5 of the Proceeds of Crime Act (POCA) 2002, under which the Crown can pursue a civil claim for the forfeiture of money that constitutes the proceeds of crime without showing that anyone has been convicted of a criminal offence (unlike confiscation under Part 2 of the same Statute). However, this provision will not normally apply where the cash is held by a defendant who has been found 'not guilty' of a crime in relation to the same money, and where such a decision would cast doubt on the acquittal (as will often be the situation in insider cases). In part, this is because the European Court of Human Rights feels that this would usually be a violation of the presumption of innocence under Article 6(2) of the European Convention on Human Rights, as was noted in judicial discussion in the Scottish case of *Scottish Ministers v Doig & Ors* [2009] CSIH 34.

As well as violating notions of double jeopardy, there are also sound practical reasons not to seek the return of innocently made profits in these situations. For example, where a broker used inside information to encourage unknowing clients to deal, the numbers involved could be vast and indeterminate.

Occasionally, it is possible that awareness that there will be no 'second bite of the cherry' may contribute to nervousness on the part of the FCA about bringing criminal prosecutions when there is the safer option of a regulatory action available.

---

55   *Daily Telegraph*, 15 November 2012.

CHAPTER 3

The Regulatory Regime

Introduction

As outlined in *Chapter 2*, insider dealing is both a criminal offence and a civil wrong. The former (the main focus of this book) can only be properly understood in the light of its close relationship to the latter, especially as the regulatory alternative has been employed almost as frequently as the criminal process to deal with such behaviour. The FSA/FCA secured the conviction of 32 people between 2008 and the end of 2016. In the same time, nearly as many individuals received 'Final Notices' (the decision of the FCA, issued at the conclusion of the regulatory enforcement process, which details the terms of statements, orders or penalties imposed) for insider dealing, although prosecutions now exceed regulatory disposals (as prosecution has taken precedence since 2008).[1] As a result, further consideration of the regulatory process is necessary, if only because it places criminal prosecution in context.

Advent of the Civil Wrong

Perhaps unusually, when it comes to the proscription of something that was once entirely legal, the introduction of civil sanctions followed (rather than preceded) the criminalisation of insider dealing by 20 years. This is

---

1   Lev Bromberg *et al*, 'The Extent and Intensity of Insider Trading Enforcement — An International Comparison', 2017, p.15. http://www.tandfonline.com/doi/abs/10.1080/14735970.2016.122395

the converse of the experience in many European and even some common law jurisdictions, such as Hong Kong. Nevertheless, since the start of the 21st-century a strong civil regulatory regime to punish insider dealing has run alongside the sanctions established by Part V of the Criminal Justice Act 1993.

Despite its relatively recent arrival, the advent of such a regime was well-heralded. The introduction of civil sanctions was proposed at several points during the 1970s. In 1990, a select committee, appointed to examine Department of Trade and Industry (DTI) investigations also recommended a system of civil penalties, albeit that the then Government dismissed its findings on the basis that insider dealing was a 'public wrong' that warranted criminal prosecution. However, throughout the following decade, informed observers continued to express doubts as to whether criminal rather than civil sanctions were best suited to combat most cases of insider dealing.[2] This became increasingly marked, as the criminal regime appeared to be a disappointment.

The Legislation

A change of government in 1997 meant that civil sanctions for insider dealing moved back on to the agenda. They were finally introduced by Part 8 of the Financial Services and Markets Act 2000 (FSMA), which is the key Statute regulating the financial services industry in the UK. Section 118(2) FSMA made insider dealing ('where an insider deals, or attempts to deal, in a qualifying investment or related investment on the basis of inside information') the first of seven forms of proscribed market abuse. The improper disclosure of inside information was the second form of abuse specified (very roughly corresponding to the criminal offence established in section 52(2) CJA 1993).

However, on 3 July 2016, the European Union's Market Abuse Regulation (MAR) 2016, which replaced MAD, came into force. MAR aims to increase market integrity and investor protection. It introduced changes to the UK civil regulatory regime via the doctrine of 'direct effect', which allows its

---

2   Keith Wotherspoon, 'Insider Dealing: The New Law: Part V of the Criminal Justice Act 1993', 1994, p.433.

provisions to be enforced immediately before national courts. Even so, the UK will also amend relevant primary and secondary legislation by statutory instrument to ensure their compatibility with the regulation. The FCA has made changes to its handbook, including the Code of Market Conduct, to ensure that its rules comply with the new regime.

Although there are some differences, MAR bears many similarities to its predecessor, so that much of the existing case law on regulatory actions will continue to be relevant. For example, the definition of 'inside information' found in Article 7 of MAR is very similar to that contained in section 118C FSMA, although slightly broader in the former (it now covers inside information for spot commodity contracts). Articles 14(a) and (b) of MAR prohibit insider dealing, including, significantly, *attempting* to engage in insider dealing (a new development) and recommending or inducing another person to engage in insider dealing. Article 14(c) of MAR prohibits a person from unlawfully disclosing inside information 'save in the normal course of his employment, profession or duties'. Article 8 of MAR has also made it clear that encouraging another person to deal on the basis of inside information amounts to unlawful disclosure of such information and (unlike under the criminal regime) that the use of inside information to amend or cancel a pre-existing order should be considered to be insider dealing. Furthermore, MAR extends the scope of the market abuse regime. 'Extra-territorial' behaviour that formerly would not have offended the UK civil regime might now be caught by it.

Standard of Proof in Regulatory Actions

In some respects, the civil regime is even more powerful now than it was just a few years ago. Initially, the Financial Services and Markets Tribunal and its successor (from 2010) the Upper Tribunal (Tax and Chancery Chamber) fell into the then widespread evidential 'heresy' of expecting an almost quasi-criminal standard of proof in insider and other market abuse cases, even though, in theory, they only had to be established to the normal civil standard. This was done by recourse to the (by then) decades old notion of a sliding scale of proof within the civil standard, depending on the gravity of the allegation being made: *Hornal v Neuberger Products Ltd.*

[1957] 1 QB 247.

Thus, in *Davidson and Tatham v The Financial Services Authority* [2006] UKFSM 031 the tribunal noted: 'These are very serious allegations [of market abuse] which will require cogent evidence to establish'. In the same year, a credit risk and treasury manager of a listed company, was initially fined £300,000 by the FSA's Regulatory Decisions Committee (RDC) for making spread bets after allegedly becoming aware of serious financial difficulties facing his employer. He referred the matter to the Financial Services and Markets Tribunal, arguing that the criminal standard of proof should apply, and this had not been satisfied in his case. This argument was held to be valid, the tribunal concluding that there could be no doubt that an allegation that an individual had been guilty of conduct for which he should be punished by the imposition of a penalty of £300,000 was a very grave charge, so that: '... compelling evidence must be adduced if it is to be established. Put it another way, if one applies the 'sliding scale' suggested in Mohammed [an earlier market abuse tribunal case], the slide must be very close to the upper end of the scale ... it is difficult to draw a meaningful distinction between the standard we must apply and the criminal standard'.[3] However, the tribunal also decided that this standard had been met in the instant case, albeit that the penalty was reduced to £250,000 (£100,000 to disgorge profits and £150,000 as an additional punitive element).[4] Slightly confusing burden and standard of proof, the Final Notice in a regulatory case from 2009, that did not go to the tribunal, observed that: 'The FSA notes that the burden of proof in a case of serious market abuse is high and that the standard of proof is on a balance of probabilities'.[5]

Arguably, both the regulator and the Upper Tribunal were rather slow to pick up on the House of Lords' rejection of the notion of 'standards within standards' in *Re B* [2009] 1 AC 11, except in cases where the sheer gravity of the allegation made it inherently more unlikely that it had occurred, as had originally been discussed in *Re H (Minors)* [1996] AC 563, or the handful of specific situations that were deemed to be *sui generis*. For example, the

---

3   *New Law Journal*, 14 March 2008.

4   *Telegraph & Argus*, 19 August 2006; FSA Final Notice, 6 October 2006.

5   FCA Final Notice, 6 October 2009.

criminal standard is applied in contempt of court cases originating in civil matters (which can result in imprisonment), the imposition of anti-social behaviour orders and serious disciplinary hearings involving lawyers: *Re a Solicitor* [1993] QB 69. (Whether the last of these should continue is currently being debated).

Somewhat belatedly, in *Ian Charles Hannam v The Financial Conduct Authority* [2014] UKUT 0233 (TCC) the Upper Tribunal concluded that cases of market abuse (including insider dealing) dealt with by the civil process did not fall into the same 'special' category as grave allegations against members of the legal profession, not least because most other professions used the ordinary civil standard, whatever the gravity of the allegation. As a result, the standard of proof in regulatory actions for insider dealing was normally a simple 'balance of probabilities' or 'more probable than not'.

As the financial penalty imposed by the FCA can include a substantial punitive element, and the regulator can prevent recipients from working in the financial services industry, some observers will still feel that the normal civil standard is too low. Perhaps significantly, in Hong Kong, a concern that the penal element present in 'severe' pecuniary fine orders could be construed as 'criminal' for human rights purposes led the territory's government to remove the power to impose them from its Market Misconduct Tribunal.[6]

However, in some cases at least, those facing such allegations will be comforted by Lord Nicholls observation in *Re H* that the: '... inherent probability or improbability of an event is itself a matter to be taken into account when weighing the probabilities and deciding whether, on balance, the event occurred'. A senior banker of unblemished reputation (for example) accused of a small scale case of insider dealing, who says that his trades were based on personal analysis of the market, might well get some evidential mileage out of this proposition.

Going to the Regulatory Decisions Committee

If, following their initial investigation, the FCA believes regulatory (but not criminal) action is justified it submits the case papers to the RDC for

---

6   Rita Cheung, 'Criminal Prosecution for Insider Dealing: A Hong Kong Perspective', 2010, p.163.

consideration. Although this body is part of the regulator, and its panel members are appointed by and accountable to the FCA board, it is operationally separate. Those members of the FCA who were involved in the initial investigation will not be involved in the RDC's decision-making process. Apart from its chairman, none of the members of the RDC is a full-time FCA employee.[7]

Normally, a group of three people sit on the RDC to consider a case. This panel is usually made up of a chair or deputy chair (there are several of the latter), drawn from lawyers of at least seven years standing, who preside individually over the process, and two lay members drawn from business, consumer and finance industry backgrounds. For example, in 2017, the latter included people of such diverse professions as John Callender, a senior commercial banker, and Dame Elizabeth Neville, a former chief constable.[8] If, however, the decision is considered to be straightforward an RDC chair or deputy can decide, on his or her own, whether to issue a statutory notice. The RDC has its own legal advisers, separate from those recommending the action. Nevertheless, it is the final stage of an administrative decision-making process, not a judicial hearing.

The RDC Decision

If, after reviewing the findings of the initial investigation, the RDC decides action is appropriate it issues a warning notice to the person under investigation pursuant to section 67(1) FSMA. This must state the amount of any financial penalty that it is minded to impose and, if the decision is to suspend or restrict their performance of a regulated function, for how long this will last. An intention to publish a statement relating to the case (usually censuring the dealer) must also set out its proposed terms: section 67(2)-(5) FSMA. The recipient of the notice may then make written or oral representations on its content to the committee. In the latter situation, a meeting is arranged between the subject of the investigation and their lawyers (if instructed) who will often have specialist experience in contesting RDC findings and negotiating settlements. The Financial Services Lawyers

---

7   Barry Rider *et al*, *Market Abuse and Insider Dealing*, 2016, p.294.

8   FCA Press Release, 24 July 2017.

Association has set up a scheme whereby specialist lawyers will provide free legal advice to those who have been referred to the RDC or appealed to the Upper Tribunal and cannot afford representation.

The representations meeting allows suspects to advance arguments against the FCA taking any action at all, and about the penalty that should be imposed if it does. Normally, the FCA's enforcement team, the RDC's legal advisers, and a case handler from the committee's secretariat will also be present. The RDC then makes its decision. Significantly more cases end by executive settlement, i.e. a formal agreement between the parties (the RDC and alleged insider dealer), than are concluded by the RDC making a unilateral decision. If the RDC decides action is not appropriate, a notice of discontinuance is issued. If action is deemed to be the correct course or is agreed upon as part of a settlement, the committee issues a Decision Notice, containing details of the proposed penalties, whether fines, suspensions from regulated activities, or public censures.

Under section 67(7) FSMA, anyone subject to an adverse Decision Notice issued by the RDC without their agreement can refer the matter to an Upper Tribunal (Tax and Chancery Chamber) hearing within 28 days of receiving it. If they fail to do this, the FCA will issue a Final Notice, which contains details about the action to be taken. If the person investigated fails to pay any financial penalty contained in such a notice, the FCA can recover the amount due as a debt owed to the regulator.[9] The FSA/FCA issued 85 Final Notices in respect of market abuse (of all types) between April 2003 and March 2015.[10]

Reference to the Upper Tribunal

If the person suspected of insider dealing exercises his or her right to refer the case to the Upper Tribunal, the RDC has 28 days to draft a statement of case explaining why it made its decision. The recipient must then submit (in writing) to the tribunal (and the FCA) an explanation of those elements of the statement that they are disputing, and why. The matter is then set

---

9   Michael Filby, 'The Enforcement of Insider Dealing under the Financial Services and Markets Act 2000', 2003, p.334.

10   *Fair and Effective Markets Review: Final Report*, 2015, London, p.85.

down for a hearing. The tribunal sits in London (for England and Wales), Edinburgh (Scotland) and Belfast (Northern Ireland) and is independent of the rest of the FCA. The hearing is not an appeal but, instead, constitutes an entirely fresh, and the first 'judicial', examination of the matter. For example, in *Timothy Edward Baldwin and WRT Investments Ltd v. Financial Services Authority* (2006) the tribunal, after a lengthy rehearing of the evidence, which included evidence from and cross-examination of expert witnesses, upheld Mr Baldwin's challenge to the earlier decision of the FSA fining him £24,000 for insider dealing, and completely dismissed the case against him.[11] As a result, judicial review of an RDC decision, rather than an appeal to the tribunal, cannot normally be brought: *R (Willford) v FSA* [2013] EWCA Civ 677.

Under section 133(4) FSMA, the tribunal may consider any evidence that is relevant to the subject matter of the reference, whether or not it was available to the RDC when it made its decision, so that entirely new material may be adduced by both sides. Like most tribunals, it is not bound by the strict rules of evidence. Typically, it will have a bench of three members, presided over by a Chamber President, who is usually a tribunal judge appointed to the Upper Tribunal (Tax and Chancery Chamber), and so normally a lawyer of at least seven years standing. Whilst some hold full-time salaried positions, most serve on a part-time, fee-paid, basis, sitting for at least 15 days each year.[12] In exceptional circumstances, such as a case of great legal complexity, the president can be drawn from the High Court bench. Thus, in the *Hannam* case it was Mr Justice Warren, a judge of the Chancery Division, who (significantly) had a circuit judge as one of his co-adjudicators.[13] The hearing is held in public unless there are special reasons for it being convened *in camera*.

---

11   Joanna Gray, *Journal of Financial Regulation & Compliance*, 2006, Vol.14(3), pp.316–320.

12   The career of Timothy Herrington provides an illustration of the background of a full-time Tribunal judge. He was made a partner at Clifford Chance in 1985, specialising in company and financial services law. On retiring from this firm in 2005, he joined the FSA, and became Chairman of the RDC. In 2012, Herrington was appointed a Judge of the Upper Tribunal (Tax and Chancery Chamber).

13   *Ian Charles Hannam –and– The Financial Conduct Authority*, Upper Tribunal (Tax and Chancery Chamber), Appeal number FS/2012/0013.

The parties are told in advance what documents they need to provide. After hearing from both sides, the Upper Tribunal usually reserves its decision, which is conveyed to the parties within three months. An alleged legal mistake by it can be taken to the Court of Appeal (in England and Wales), with the former's permission or, if this is not forthcoming, that of the latter. However, appeals based on claims that the Upper Tribunal made errors of fact (rather than law) or reached unacceptable factual conclusions are exceptionally difficult to sustain.

It should be noted that although previous regulatory findings are not convictions, they are capable, in appropriate circumstances, of being evidence of 'bad character' for the purposes of section 101 of the Criminal Justice Act (CJA) 2003 should, for example, the recipient be prosecuted subsequently in a criminal forum for a similar offence and his or her previous conduct becomes relevant to the case in hand (propensity evidence, etc.). This might be because the evidence on which they were based revealed the commission of an offence (although the prosecution route was not taken) or would be deemed to be some other form of 'reprehensible conduct' under section 112 CJA 2003. Of course, this would have to be proved at trial by adducing admissible evidence (the regulatory finding not being a conviction).

Regulatory Penalties

The penalties imposed via the regulatory process can be severe, if not positively draconian. Section 123 FSMA allows the FCA to impose an unlimited fine, 'such amount as it considers appropriate', where it is satisfied that someone has engaged in market abuse, including insider dealing. This means that regulatory fines do not necessarily lead solely to the disgorgement of abusive profits, but can include a significant punitive element; occasionally, where there has been serious misconduct, this is several times larger than the disgorgement. As already noted, the FCA also has the power to suspend a dealer from conducting regulated activities, permanently if it deems it necessary, and to censure him or her publicly.

The FSA's first civil insider dealing case was completed almost two years after the 2000 Act came into force and was relatively minor and straightforward. In April 2002, the secretary of a modestly sized AIM-listed publisher, sold 70,000 of his own shares in the company when he became aware that it was about to issue a profits warning, so avoiding a loss of £6,825. The FSA fined him £15,000.[14] More serious cases, with much higher punishments, followed. In 2010, one man was fined £967,005 by the regulator for insider dealing.[15] In 2014 the tribunal imposed a penalty of £450,000 on an investment banker, for improper disclosure of what constituted inside information in two emails sent in furtherance of a client's commercial interests.[16] Many observers felt that this was a particularly harsh disposal, given that there was absolutely no suggestion that the disclosures had been made dishonestly or that he was not a fit person to operate in the financial markets.[17] Most dramatically, in early-2012, an American hedge fund manager was fined £3,368,000 under section 118(2) FSMA (now replaced by MAR) by the FSA for trading on inside information, although he had expressly asked not to be 'wall crossed' (the act of making a person an insider by providing them with inside information) and received the relevant information on the stated understanding that he was not being made an insider. The regulator accepted that the hedge fund manager had not knowingly and deliberately traded on inside information: '[He] did not believe that the information that he had received was inside information, and he did not intend to commit market abuse'. (It must be stressed that the fund manager remains adamant that the FSA's interpretation of the law in his case was mistaken).[18]

Much more modestly, in 2009, two bond managers were merely censured, rather than being fined or suspended. They had sold Barclays' bonds while knowing that more favourably priced bonds from the same issuer would soon come out. (The counter-parties/purchasers had lost $66,000 when this occurred and subsequently complained). However, the two men (who did not make any money personally from the trade) were adamant that they were acting in accordance with then debt market practice in selling after merely being 'sounded-out' on a new issue, and the regulator accepted

14   *The Guardian*, 8 July 2004.

15   FSA Final Notice, 12 February 2010; *The Daily Telegraph*, 16 February 2010.

16   FCA, Final Notice, No. ICH01012, 17 July 2014.

17   *Daily Telegraph*, 3 April 2012.

18   *Daily Telegraph*, 25 January 2012. FSA Final Notice, 15 February 2012.

that they quite genuinely believed that their behaviour did not constitute insider dealing.[19]

This case, like that involving the hedge fund manager (above) also reiterates that it is the statutory/legal definition, not personal belief/understanding or market practice, which always decides the issue. (The same applies to criminal prosecutions under the CJA 1993).

19   *The Guardian*, 7 October 2009; FCA Final Notice, 6 October 2009.

CHAPTER 4

The Criminal Offences

Preliminary Matters

The criminal offences relating to insider dealing are complicated, and the leading practitioner texts should be consulted to secure more than the following general outline. However, a number of important preliminary points can usefully be made immediately, to facilitate comprehension, before dealing with them more methodically.

No Need for a Tangible Benefit

There is no *requirement* for a benefit to accrue to the insider dealer as a result of his or her trading. As early as 1976, the City Company Law Committee recommended that if insider dealing was criminalised the: '... actual making [of] a profit or avoiding a loss should not be a necessary constituent of the offence'.[1] This is certainly the case under the Criminal Justice Act 1993. As soon as a deal occurs, in appropriate circumstances, the offence is committed, irrespective of its consequences. For example, in 2016, a man pleaded guilty to two counts of insider dealing in energy companies. However, the trade in only one of them made a profit. The second, a deal made in a PLC in October 2011, ahead of price-sensitive news, actually made a loss of £10,000, the market failing to react as expected and other events making

---

1   Anon, *Insider Dealing*, 1976, p.8.

their influence felt.[2] (Transaction costs can also be significant). Even so, in the circumstances of this trade, an offence had been committed. Indeed, there is no need for the inside information that prompted the deal to be publicly released; for example, where the authors of a proposed company takeover change their minds about a bid at the last moment, after an insider has traded in anticipation of just such an occurrence, although prosecutions in such situations are very rare.

Natural Persons

Currently, only 'natural' legal persons can commit the crime of insider dealing. The use of the word 'individual' in section 52 CJA 1993 and its normal legal definition precludes corporate liability (including that of public authorities), although, in theory, it seems that a company could be guilty of the secondary offence of encouraging another person to deal (or analogous offences, including what are usually termed inchoate offences).[3] This interpretation also accords with the ordinary and everyday meaning attributed to the word 'individual'.

However, in June 2015 the *Fair and Effective Markets Review* (FEMR) proposed that the regime should be extended to apply criminal liability to firms involved in insider dealing, where appropriate, as is currently the case with regard to market manipulation, if only to ensure a consistent approach.[4] In practice, making firms liable might also encourage their directors to put in place effective checks and controls on individual employees and working practices, and encourage the installation of company-wide safeguards.

Absence of Dishonesty

Although 'dishonesty' is usually present in insider dealing cases (as judicial comment regularly reiterates), the prosecution does *not* have to establish it as part of the crime's *mens rea*. As Lady Justice Arden observed in an *obiter* comment in *Ivey v Genting Casino UK Limited* [2016] EWCA Civ 1093, although: 'Parliament has made insider dealing a criminal offence ... There

---

2   FCA Press Release, 21 December 2016; Bloomberg, 21 December 2016.

3   Barry Rider *et al, Market Abuse and Insider Dealing*, 2016, p.52.

4   *Fair and Effective Markets Review: Final Report*, 2015, London, p.88.

is no requirement for dishonesty'. As a result, it is a form of strict liability offence.[5] In this, insider dealing is unlike theft, receiving, and some other fraud offences, which are subject to the test set out in *R v Ghosh* [1982] EWCA Crim 2, in which a two-limb general test for dishonesty was formulated in English law. The first limb is objective: was what the defendant did dishonest by the ordinary standards of reasonable and honest people? The second is subjective: did the defendant realise that what he or she was doing was dishonest by the standards of reasonable and honest people?

In light of the absence of a need for dishonesty in insider dealing, it would not matter if a defendant with a cynical view of The City (or perhaps one rooted in mid-20th-century practice in The Square Mile) genuinely thought that such dealing was entirely normal and correct behaviour. Indeed, in *R v Asif Nazir Butt* [2006] 2 Cr. App R (S.) 44, the applicant, the former vice-president of compliance at Credit Suisse First Boston, like the four other defendants, claimed that he did not know that what he was doing was an offence because he honestly (if mistakenly) believed that he had discovered a lacuna in the law governing the subject. As the trial judge, His Honour Judge Christopher Elwen, directed the jury, even if accepted, this did not provide a defence: 'It is unlawful and his belief, however honest you think it may be, is not a defence to the charges alleged'.[6] This has been reiterated more recently with regard to a foreign suspect who was, apparently, unaware that any aspect of the practice of insider dealing was unlawful.

Now that the regime set out in the CJA 1993 has been supplemented by the civil regulatory controls on insider dealing initially contained in the Financial Services and Markets Act (FSMA) 2000, and presently found in their replacement in the MAR 2016, it is at least arguable that there is cause to redefine the criminal offence so that it *requires* dishonesty and thus acquires a more serious *mens rea* than its regulatory counterpart.[7]

---

5   David Kirk, 'Enforcement of Criminal Sanctions for Market Abuse: Practicalities, Problem Solving and Pitfalls', 2016, p.318.

6   *The Independent*, 21 December 2004.

7   Jonathan Barnard, 'Insider Trading: An Easy Offence to Commit', 2011, p.11.

Fraud Act 2006

In theory, it is possible that some instances of insider dealing could be indicted under section 4 of the Fraud Act 2006, under which an offence can be committed by an abuse of position by those who: occupy a position in which they are expected to safeguard the financial interests of another person; dishonestly abuse that position; and intend, by means of that abuse to make a profit for themselves. However, such a prosecution does require dishonesty to be established on the part of the offender, perhaps helping to explain why they have not yet taken place.[8]

The Three Offences

The three current insider dealing criminal offences are set out in section 52 of the CJA 1993. Section 52(1) creates the basic or 'primary' dealing offence, and provides that an individual who has information as an insider is guilty of the crime if he deals in securities on a regulated market that are price-affected in relation to that information.

Section 52(2) creates two 'secondary' crimes. The first of these, in section 52(2)(a), the 'tipping' offence, occurs where an insider encourages another person to deal in price-affected securities. Although it must occur in circumstances where the insider doing the encouraging knows or has reasonable cause to believe that unlawful dealing will take place, it is not a 'result' crime (one that is only complete if and when the posited outcome materialises) and, in theory, takes place as soon as the encouragement itself occurs, although prosecuted offences committed without subsequent dealing are (unsurprisingly) extremely rare (or harder to prove). Nevertheless, encouraging a young child to deal would probably not be an offence, as the insider could not reasonably believe that they would go on to trade in shares. The offence does not require the actual passing of inside information as part of the encouragement (although this will often occur, if only to explain it), merely urging others to trade as a *result* of the inside information that the 'encourager' possesses. If the recipients of such encouragement do not know it is based on inside information they will not commit an offence

---

8   Paul Barnes, 'Insider Dealing and Market Abuse: The UK's Record on Enforcement', 2011, p.178.

if they then deal in response to it.[9] This explains why in 2012 a guilty plea to a section 52(2)(a) allegation was not inconsistent with the subsequent acquittal on section 52(1) counts of those he had been encouraged to trade, and even though they had then gone on to do so.

The second offence, set out in section 52(2)(b), occurs when an individual who has information as an insider discloses that information, other than in the proper performance of his or her employment or profession, to another person. Again, there is no requirement that actual dealing results from the disclosure. Furthermore, there is no need for any personal interest on the part of the informant in disclosing such information. In one old case, price-sensitive information was, apparently, disclosed to friends merely to explain the insider's late arrival at a wedding-party. In others, disclosure was made to impress girlfriends or colleagues.[10]

For a hypothetical example there can be considered the situation in which X, a director at Y PLC, has a whisky-fuelled lunch with Z. X tells Z that his company has just received a takeover offer that is at a considerable premium to its current share price and has yet to be made public. X *may* have committed an offence under section 52(2)(b) of the Act (although he would, presumably, avail himself of the defence contained in section 53(3) (a): see below).

This crime (disclosure) is not indicted very frequently, not least because the regulator appears to be sensitive to how draconian it might be if misapplied. Drunkenly leaking a takeover at a social event is not quite the same as compromising the security of the D-Day landings. However, it might be prosecuted in circumstances where a disclosure, but not active encouragement, that has then led to the commission of a section 52(1) offence, can be established. For example, in November 2016, a former business analyst pleaded guilty to two section 52(2)(b) counts of illegal disclosure of information relating to the IT consultancy's £1.7bn takeover. His neighbour pleaded guilty to a section 52(1) offence after admitting that he had used the information supplied by the analyst to make over £100,000 on a share

---

9   Brian McDonnell, *A Practitioner's Guide to Inside Information*, 2012, pp.226–227.

10   Barry Rider *et al*, *Market Abuse and Insider Dealing*, 2016, p.7.

deal.[11] In June 2017, a former UBS compliance officer was charged by the FCA with disclosing information relating to shares in various companies to a day trader, who allegedly went on to deal on five occasions between June 2013 and June 2014, other than in the proper performance of her employment. (The prosecution was at a very early stage at the time of writing).[12]

Interpretation of Section 52

The terms employed in section 52 are defined within sections 54 to 60 of the CJA 1993 and in Schedule 2 to the same Statute (Section 53 deals with defences). Interpreting these definitions is fundamental to understanding the offences. Unfortunately, drafting a viable crime of insider dealing that is readily comprehensible has proved enormously difficult, all over the world, and there has been no exception in UK. Indeed, a feeling that it was almost impossible to do this contributed to the introduction of the civil regulatory regime in 2000.

In July 1979, Sir Reginald Edwin Eyre noted in a House of Commons debate that he accepted the need for legislation against insider dealing, *provided* that satisfactory answers could be found to the 'difficult problems of definition' that would be entailed. Whether this requirement can be met in an entirely satisfactory manner has been a vexed question ever since. Although the CJA 1993 is widely (and rightly) thought to have simplified UK law on insider trading, it remains a very complicated crime. David Kirk (former Chief Criminal Counsel to the regulator) has described interpreting the Statute's terms and definitions as a '... world of smoke and mirrors in which the meanings of words are exposed to ever more intensive scrutiny'.[13] More is often required of the ordinary good sense of the jury than is, perhaps, entirely desirable. Key words employed in the 1993 Statute create potential problems, even allowing for assistance from the various canons of statutory interpretation and the aids set out in the Interpretation Act 1978.

Unfortunately, and at first sight perhaps surprisingly, there is a relative

---

11   FCA Press Release, 30 November 2016.

12   *Financial Times*, June 8 2017.

13   David Kirk, 'Enforcement of Criminal Sanctions for Market Abuse: Practicalities, Problem Solving and Pitfalls', 2016, p.314.

dearth of appellate level case law in this area. The only Supreme Court decisions involving insider dealing under the 1993 Act have involved other types of legal issue: *Patel v Mirza* [2016] 3 WLR 399 and *R v Rollins* [2010] UKSC 39. Even Court of Appeal decisions are rare. There are several possible reasons for this. Most importantly, defendants only rarely take issue with the wording of the Statute (rather than the facts alleged against them). As a result, the interpretation of many aspects of this complicated area of the law is reliant on purely persuasive authority from first instance decisions in the Crown Court.

Nevertheless, one reason that the criminal law governing insider dealing has remained viable over the last decade, despite apparent ambiguities in the CJA 1993 and an increasing number of prosecutions, can be found in judicial attitudes towards the enabling Statute. The courts have usually been reluctant to adopt an overly technical interpretation, one that could render its provisions ineffectual. Instead, they have adopted a purposive approach.[14] This was also found, to some degree, with its statutory predecessor. In *AG's Ref (No 1 of 1988)* [1989] 2 WLR 729 the defendant was accused of insider dealing under the Company Securities (Insider Dealing) Act 1985. At trial he was acquitted of 'obtaining' the relevant information, the judge finding that he had done nothing positive to acquire it, rather than receiving it as an unsolicited gift. The House of Lords, which considered the White Paper that preceded the 1980 legislation on insider dealing and the reason for the legislation (preventing such dealing), decided that: '… if one construes the key word "obtained" in the light of the purpose behind the Act, the conclusion must, in our judgment, be that it means no more than "received"'. (The court also noted that Lord Diplock had observed, in *Black-Clawson International Ltd. v. Papierwerke Waldhof-Aschaffenburg AG* [1975] AC 591, that White Papers could be used for identifying this purpose). In *R v Staines and Morrisey* [1997] 2 Cr App R 426, another insider case decided under the 1985 Act, the Lord Chief Justice, Lord Bingham, expressly noted that it was 'important to bear in mind the mischief at which the legislation is aimed'. On this basis, it could be argued that the 1993 Statute set out to deal with

---

14   Clare Montgomery *et al, Fraud: Criminal Law and Procedure*, 2015, at D.5.01–05.

insider dealing more efficiently, and the courts are merely producing rulings that will bring this about, as occurred in a very different (and much more clear-cut) context in *Smith v Hughes* [1960] 2 All ER 859.

However, some might argue that the increase in convictions for insider dealing under the 1993 Act over the past decade has been secured by pushing this approach to its limits, especially as it is not clear that it was Parliament's intention to catch large numbers of (potentially) peripherally involved secondary insiders. The relative dearth of insider prosecutions for the 15 years after 1993 was not purely down to a lack of will on the part of the regulator. It reflected a real appreciation of the difficulties such cases posed as the law stood, if it were strictly interpreted.

Elements of the Offence

The essential requirements for the section 52(1) offence to be made out are that:

(a)   a person must have information as an insider; and

(b)   they must deal in securities that are price-affected in relation to that information.[15]

Expanding on this, a defendant is guilty (subject to defences) of insider dealing if he or she deals, in appropriate circumstances (with regard to territoriality, type of security, etc.), when he or she has information that is, and he or she knows is, inside information (with regard to being suitably specific, precise, price-sensitive, etc.), and he or she has it, and knows that he or she has it, from an inside source: section 57(1)(a)-(b) CJA 1993 (paraphrased).

However, it is easier to understand the crime if it is broken down into its smallest constituent elements. In simplistic terms, for an offence to be made out the accused person must:

(1)   deal in;

(2)   specified securities; on

(3)   specified markets; while

(4)   in or connected to the UK in some way; as

---

15   Barry Rider *et al*, *Market Abuse and Insider Dealing*, 2016, p.54.

(5) an insider; and

(6) in possession of inside information.

Part (1) of these prerequisites has be modified to reflect the requirements of the first of the section 52(2) secondary offences. These six elements will be dealt with in turn.

Dealing

Under section 55(1) of the CJA 1993, 'dealing in securities' is broadly defined, consisting of, *inter alia*, acquiring or disposing of the securities (whether as principal or agent), or procuring, directly or indirectly, an acquisition or disposal of the securities by any other person. Thus, instructing a professional intermediary, such as a share trader or stockbroker, or telling someone else (whether a friend or an accountant) to instruct a broker to make a share purchase or sale on your behalf, are as much insider dealing as personally buying or selling shares. Furthermore, in many situations the insider to such a transaction can be indicted as a secondary party to the section 52(1) offence, even though he or she does not personally deal. For example, in the *Uberoi* case (see *Chapter 2*), the Crown Court accepted that it was appropriate to charge the accused with allegedly aiding and abetting the dealing of his father, rather than alleging procurement or a section 52(2) offence.[16]

However, it seems that there must be active 'dealing', that is buying or selling, or 'acquisition or disposal' to quote the Statute; the Crown cannot accuse a defendant of *refraining* from trading in stocks or other securities as a result of inside information. For example, suppose A has decided to offload a tranche of shares in B PLC and ordered his stockbroker to do this, but, just before this goes through, becomes aware (as an insider) of an imminent takeover bid for the company which will drive up its share price. He cancels the order to sell the shares. No offence is committed.[17] By contrast, the civil wrong, now governed by Article 8.1 MAR 2016, makes clear that the use of inside information to amend or cancel an order where the order was placed before the person concerned possessed the inside information *is* considered

---

16   Ibid, p.56.

17   Karen Anderson *et al, A Practitioner's Guide to the Law and Regulation of Market Abuse*, 2017, p.67.

insider dealing but, of course, this does not affect the criminal regime.

The Securities

The Statute extends to deals using inside information relating to most but not all types of securities. Under section 54(1) of the CJA 1993 it only applies to those that fall within Schedule 2 (which may be amended by statutory order) and which also satisfy any other conditions made by the Treasury. The securities listed include shares, warrants, debt securities, options, futures, gilts, depository receipts, local authority stock, and contracts for difference.

Whether spread-bets fall under the definition of 'securities' for the purposes of section 54 is an interesting question. They were of marginal significance when the CJA 1993 was drafted, and so were not specifically referred to in the Statute, and the Treasury has not sought to amend Schedule 2 to include them in the years since. Even so, in 2004, it was ruled by His Honour Judge Elwen, presiding over the trial in *Butt*, that they did fall under the definition (to an extent, they resemble futures and options). Perhaps unfortunately, but not untypically in this area of the law, this point was not subsequently appealed despite a conviction ensuing, and has not been contested in any case since. Most academic and practitioner observers share Judge Elwen's analysis. For example, Barry Rider feels that the 'better view' is that they are covered by the legislation.[18] However, cynics might view it as another indication of the courts adopting a highly purposive approach to the legislation. Arguably, the Statute should be amended to cover them, if only for the avoidance of doubt.

When the Bank of England published its *Fair and Effective Markets Review* in June 2015, it proposed that criminal sanctions for market abuse by both individuals and firms should extend to a wider range of fixed income, currency, and commodity instruments than is currently contained in the CJA 1993, if only to keep up with market developments and innovations.[19]

---

18   Barry Rider *et al*, *Market Abuse and Insider Dealing*, 2016, p.54.

19   *Fair and Effective Markets Review: Final Report*, 2015, p.88.

Designated Markets

The insider deal has to take place on a designated 'regulated market' or through a professional intermediary to be prosecuted. (Although the phrase 'regulated market' is also used in MAR, there are important differences between the two regimes in this respect). Numerous markets, both at home and abroad, in addition to the LSE's Main Market and Alternative Investment Market are identified for the purposes of Part V of the CJA, so that insider dealing on them can be a crime. They include all UK and most major EU stock exchanges, and some from further afield, as well as many other markets, extending to such diverse institutions as the Milan Stock Exchange, OMLX, NASDAQ, *Nouveau Marche*, the London Securities and Derivatives Exchange, the Vienna Stock Exchange, along with dozens of others listed in the schedule to the Insider Dealing (Securities and Markets) Order 1994 (SI 1994/1870).[20]

This list has been amended and updated periodically by statutory instruments over the past 20 years as markets have come and gone, in what is often largely a renaming process. Among them, and for example, was the Insider Dealing (Securities and Regulated Markets) (Amendment) Order 2000, which added three markets (OFEX, COREDEAL, and the Brussels based EASDAQ) to the list, thereby bringing the securities traded on these exchanges under the jurisdiction of the CJA 1993 for the purposes of insider dealing. At the same time, the Securities Exchange of Iceland was removed from the list, because it was already there as the Iceland Stock Exchange (a simple error but perhaps indicative of the speed with which such markets change).[21] Similarly, the Insider Dealing (Securities and Regulated Markets) (Amendment) Order 2002 which was made on 18th July 2002, came into force the following day, and provided, *inter alia*, that when it came to Article 10 of the 1994 order: '… for "Tradepoint Financial Networks plc", substitute "virt-x Exchange Limited"'.

However, purely private trading, or trading on a market that is not identified in the Statute, even if it involves securities that are covered by Schedule

---

20 Karen Anderson *et al*, *A Practitioner's Guide to the Law and Regulation of Market Abuse*, 2017, pp.28–29.

21 Hansard, HL Deb 14 July 2000, Vol. 615, cc550–2.

2 of the CJA 1993 and occurs against a backdrop of insider information, is likely to be outside the scope of the offence, *unless* it occurs through a professional intermediary. Thus, over-the-counter (OTC) transactions, carried out using insider information, such as a contract for difference (CFD) priced by reference to a company's share price, and entered into with a financial institution, such as a bank, that constitutes a professional intermediary, *would* still be covered.[22]

Territorial Scope

Under section 62(1) CJA 1993 an individual is not guilty of an offence falling under section 52(1) of the Act unless the crime that it is alleged he or she committed has some territorial connection with the United Kingdom. This reflects the age-old principle that the basis of English criminal jurisdiction is to maintain the Sovereign's peace within the Realm. It means that: the defendant must have been within the UK at the time when he or she is alleged to have done any act constituting, or forming part of, the alleged dealing and the market on which the dealing is alleged to have occurred is regulated in the United Kingdom; or, alternatively, a professional intermediary was within the United Kingdom at the time when he or she is alleged to have done anything by means of which the offence was committed. Case law suggests that this requirement cannot be circumvented by alleging that an individual who does not meet any of these requirements was in a joint-enterprise with someone who did.[23]

Nevertheless, and to consider a straightforward example, if A telephones his or her London broker from Monte Carlo, asking them to make what is (unbeknown to the broker) an inside trade on the LSE, he or she is committing a section 52(1) offence. Similarly, if an insider in Leeds telephones a broker in Frankfurt telling the broker to buy certain shares on the *Deutsche Bourse*, he or she will be committing the same offence.[24]

Under section 62(2), an individual is not guilty of an offence falling

---

22 Karen Anderson *et al, A Practitioner's Guide to the Law and Regulation of Market Abuse*, 2017, pp.29–30.

23 Barry Rider *et al, Market Abuse and Insider Dealing*, 2016, p.70.

24 Brian McDonnell, *A Practitioner's Guide to Inside Information*, 2012, p.240.

within section 52(2) CJA 1993 (encouraging or disclosing) unless either: he or she was within the United Kingdom at the time when he or she is alleged to have disclosed the information or encouraged the dealing; or the alleged recipient of the information or encouragement was within the United Kingdom at the time when he or she is alleged to have received the information or encouragement.

Insiders

Under section 57(1) of the CJA 1993 a person has information as an insider only if: it is inside information (see below); has received it from an inside source; and 'knows' the first two prerequisites apply. Thus, it normally has to be established that, at the time he or she chose to deal, they understood the specificity and materiality of the non-public information in his or her possession and that it came from someone with an inside position or, alternatively, a 'tippee' who had the information directly or indirectly from someone who was in that position.[25]

Trading as a result of inside information without being aware of its provenance is not a crime. Reportedly, James Sanders, the director of a brokerage firm, not only traded personally on inside information received from a relative, but also advised his clients to do so on the basis of that information, without revealing it, so committing offences under both section 52(1) and 52(2)(a). The clients, who were unaware as to why their professional adviser was advising them to buy certain shares (they would have assumed it was his business acumen), did not commit any offence, even though it ultimately made them millions of pounds in profits. Clearly, 'knowledge' is a key concept in the Act *both* with regard to the type of information and its source; it will be dealt with here, but the points raised apply equally to the type of information.

Knowledge

Obviously, 'knowledge' must be much more than an awareness of vague rumours. More significantly, and much more problematically, in English

---

25   Keith Wotherspoon, 'Insider Dealing: The New Law: Part V of the Criminal Justice Act 1993', 1994, p.428.

law it is usually taken to mean more than 'belief', which is expressly used for the mental element of many other criminal offences. For example, section 22 of the Theft Act 1968 provides that a person handles stolen goods if he or she 'knows *or* believes' them to be stolen. In *R v Hall* (1985) 81 Cr App R 260, the Court of Appeal held that 'belief' was something short of knowledge, and applied to the situation where a person could not say for certain that the goods they received were stolen, but there was no other reasonable conclusion in the light of all the circumstances. This is itself a very high mental state, and was expressly distinguished by Mr Justice Boreham from mere suspicion: 'I suspect that these goods may be stolen, but it may be on the other hand that they are not'. Belief is expressed as an alternative mental state to knowledge in a significant number of other Statutes, such as witness intimidation contrary to section 51(1) of the Criminal Justice and Public Order Act 1994, which is committed 'knowing or believing that the victim is assisting in the investigation of an offence'. It was open to those drafting the provisions for Parliament to stipulate belief as an acceptable alternative to knowledge for insider dealing under the 1993 Act; they did not do so.

Taken to a strict conclusion, deeming a strong belief to be inadequate to establish knowledge would create serious problems, especially in prosecutions involving secondary insiders. Sarah Clarke has noted that there is some (albeit very limited) authority for the notion that *actual* knowledge might not be necessary, and that it could extend to wilfully shutting one's eyes to the truth. Although it might be argued that such an interpretation would risk drifting into mere 'belief', this analysis is reasonable, *provided* it is confined to covering the proverbial 'nudge, nudge, wink, wink' type situation.[26] In *Westminster City Council v Croyalgrange Limited* [1986] 1 WLR 674, Lord Bridge observed that it was always open to the tribunal of fact to: '... base a finding of knowledge on evidence that the defendant had deliberately shut his eyes to the obvious or refrained from inquiry because he suspected the truth but did not wish to have his suspicion confirmed'. However, the reference to 'evidence' in this context is significant. A reading of numerous authorities on this issue reinforces the notion that for this type

---

26   Sarah Clarke, *Insider Dealing: Law and Practice*, 2013, p.88.

of constructive knowledge to be present the evidence in question must be quite compelling and unequivocal.

It does not help with the much more common scenario in which 'someone in the city' gives investment advice to a colleague, friend or family member without going into the precise basis for (or source of) his or her opinion. When giving evidence, an (acquitted) trader, who was a defendant in a modern insider dealing trial, reportedly claimed that in his world it was an unspoken rule never to ask the source of a tip, so that 'In every rumo[u]r there is uncertainty'.[27] The recipient might 'suspect' or even 'believe' that it was founded on inside information, but they would not usually 'know' that to be the case. There would often be a not insignificant chance that the tip was the result of legitimate analysis and judgment (or even 'ramping'). Although, in *obiter* comments in *Miller v Ministry of Pensions*, [1947] 2 All ER 372, Mr Justice Denning (as he then was) felt that proving something beyond reasonable doubt did not extend to negating 'fanciful possibilities', such an eventuality will often be too likely to be dismissed on this basis. Arguably, to prevent the Statute failing in certain situations, and the mischief that it was aimed at going without a remedy, the courts have sometimes stretched the meaning of 'know' into 'strong belief'. It might, instead, be better to expressly amend the 1993 Act to include 'belief' (or accept more acquittals and non-prosecutions on this basis).

Inside Source

A defendant has information from an inside source only if he or she has acquired it through: being a director, employee, or shareholder of an issuer of securities; having access to the information by virtue of his or her employment, office or profession; or (vitally) the 'direct or indirect source' of his or her information is a person within one of the above categories (and the recipient knows it).

Thus, and obviously, a company director (whether executive or non-executive) who is negotiating a takeover is an insider, as are the (independent) solicitor and accountant who provide legal and financial advice on the deal,

---

27   *Bloomberg Businessweek*, 28 June 2016.

and even the secretary in an office or a worker in the print-room who keep their eyes open for interesting documents and read, copy, or download a briefing paper on the pending transaction (as occurred in *R v Mustafa and Others* in 2012).[28] The meaning of 'shareholders' is self-explanatory; although price-sensitive information is only rarely disseminated to all the shareholders in a company, individual major investors are sometimes consulted on important decisions. These groups might be termed 'primary' insiders, because of their position in, or professional relationship to, the relevant company.[29]

However, and vitally, a person who is totally unconnected to the company also has information as an insider *if* he or she obtains it from one of the above, knowing about the provenance of the information they have supplied. Effectively, they then become 'contaminated' by their insider status. This massively expands the potential pool of insiders. The recipients of such information are sometimes referred to as 'secondary' insiders and would also commit an offence under section 52(1) CJA 1993 if they then dealt on the basis of that information. They would *still* be guilty if they learnt about such information at one or more steps removed from the primary insider or inside source *provided* they 'knew' where it originated, as section 57(2)(b) refers to receiving it from a 'direct or *indirect*' source (emphasis added), albeit that this is something that will get progressively harder to establish in a forensic environment with each extra link in the chain. Furthermore, where information has passed through several links it may have lost precision and/or specificity (see below) making it increasingly difficult to prove that the eventual tippee has insider information.[30]

For example, in a case from 2010 each of two suspects were secondary insiders because the original tip they used came from someone (never identified) inside the firm one of them had retired from some years earlier, going from him via one of the two men to his colleague. Similarly, in the case involving Miranda and James Sanders, tried in 2012, the inside information came from a relative who was supplying confidential information overheard from her husband, who was head of mergers and acquisitions

28 *Daily Telegraph*, 27 July 2012.

29 Barry Rider *et al*, *Market Abuse and Insider Dealing*, 2016, pp.4–5.

30 Ibid, 2016, p.76.

for the accountants involved in each of the relevant takeover deals (He had no knowledge of his wife's activity).[31]

This situation is similar to the current regulatory regime. Article 8.4 of MAR, having mentioned management, shareholders, professional advisers, and employees, notes that insider status also extends to anyone else who possesses inside information who 'knows or ought to know that it is inside information'. However, the crime does not include those who have constructive knowledge ('ought to know') of the information's provenance.

Perhaps significantly, it seems that it can be inferred that a defendant in a criminal case had acquired their information from an inside source simply by dint of their situation, and especially their close contact with, or proximity to, insiders. In the 2016 prosecution of Manjeet Singh Mohal, Andrew Marshall, counsel for the FCA, informed an Old Bailey jury that: 'The prosecution case is that when you look at the evidence, there's clear evidence that he [Mohal] must have obtained inside information and that he then disclosed it to Reshim Birk'. Although Mohal had worked at Logica for a decade as a business analyst, he was not included on its formal list of insiders on the takeover that constituted the inside information in this case, albeit relatively intimate with those who were. Marshall also told the jury that: 'We can't say precisely how he got that information. We don't have to prove it either'. Unfortunately for legal observers (but not for human integrity), Mohal subsequently changed his plea to 'guilty'.[32]

Inside Information

'Inside information' is another key concept in the Statute, and defined in section 56(1)-(2) CJA 1993, whose terms largely mirror those contained in the EU's Insider Dealing Directive of 1989. They are broadly similar to (but not the same as) those found in the civil market abuse regime now contained in the MAR 2016.

Section 56 provides a four-fold test, stating that inside information is material that: relates to particular securities or to a particular issuer or issuers of securities, and not to securities or issuers of securities generally; is

---

31   *The Guardian*, 20 June 2012. This case was the first FSA/SEC joint investigation.

32   *Financial Times*, 29 November 2016.

specific or precise; has not been made public; and, if it were made public, would be likely to have a significant effect on the price of any securities. In theory, there should be considerable scope for the definition of all of these terms to become legal issues at trial. Nevertheless, such cases are much less common than might be expected.

Particular

Under section 56(1)(a) the inside information must relate to *particular* securities. In *R v Staines and Morrisey* [1997] 2 Cr App R 426, a case decided under the 1985 Act, the Lord Chief Justice, Lord Bingham accepted as correct the trial judge's direction that inside information of something like (for example) a takeover bid must normally be sufficient to identify the company to which it was related. However, the company did not have to be named expressly. It would be sufficient if enough clues were given to allow the recipient to identify it without significant additional information. The type of company, its price to earnings ratio, and approximate share price might, together, be enough, merely requiring access to a financial newspaper and an ability to join the dots on the part of the recipient. Doubtless this is still good law under the 1993 Act.

It should be noted that section 60(4) CJA 1993 states that information will be treated as relating to a company: '... not only where it is about the company but also where it may affect the company's business prospects'. This is potentially fairly broad. Suppose that a relatively small company, A PLC, is dependent for most of its work on a much larger company, B PLC, that is about to be subject to a takeover bid by another large (but similar) company, C PLC, that has its own sources for what is provided/produced by A, so that it is likely to rationalise its supply chains by dropping A after the takeover. The announcement of the bid will very probably have a major impact on A's shares, and until it is publicly released may be 'inside information' for that company, just as it is for B PLC, i.e. someone who was aware of it who sold a tranche of shares in A before it was made public could be guilty of insider dealing.

Very importantly, information that might damage a company's business prospects will not be 'inside' if it affects securities (or their issuers) *generally*.

An insider will not commit an offence if they pass on information that affects the entire market that a company operates in, however confidential it might be. This would cover the (admittedly rather implausible) situation in which A, the chairman of B PLC, announces to C that he has been told by the Governor of the Bank of England that there would be a very major rise in interest rates the following week, something that will almost certainly send the entire stock market tumbling. C, the insider recipient, sells his share portfolio (including shares in B PLC) in anticipation of this occurring, and escapes a major loss. No offence has been committed, seemingly.

However, the inside information does not have to refer to a single company. Section 56(1)(a) makes it clear that it can refer to 'particular issuers of securities'. The use of the plural suggests that it could be 'sector-wide', relating to an industry in which a specific company operates.[33] There is, inevitably, an issue as to how particular 'particular' must be. Suppose the director of a warplane manufacturing company purchased shares in his or her own company after being told by a Minister that it was to become government policy to increase armaments spending or, even more specifically, to concentrate defence spending on the air-force? Would this be sufficiently 'particular'? Would it extend to something that affected: all companies engaged in extracting raw materials; all metal mining companies; just iron ore mining companies; or purely iron ore mining companies operating in Western Australia?

To consider a 'drawn from life' situation, on 29 August 2017, shares in each of the major British grocers (Tesco, Sainsbury, Morrison, etc.) fell by up to 2.6 per cent after Amazon purchased a large whole foods business and immediately decided to slash prices.[34] Ignoring the fact that the decline was probably far too small to suggest that the information about Amazon's plans would have had a 'significant' impact on UK grocers' share prices (see below), would it, in any event, have been sufficiently specific to constitute inside information if someone who owned shares in a major grocer became aware of it before it was announced and disposed of them prior to the news being made public?

---

33 Barry Rider *et al, Market Abuse and Insider Dealing*, 2016, pp.58–59.
34 *Daily Telegraph*, 29 August 2017.

Authority on this issue is limited. However, in 1996, an individual was acquitted of insider dealing having been apprised of what might be termed 'sector-wide' information. In June 1994, the electricity regulator, had written to the directors of the dozen UK regional electricity companies setting out proposals for price controls in the industry. These were more favourable to the companies than had been widely anticipated. The individual, a director of strategy at one of the electricity companies, subsequently invested a small amount of money in a rival. When the electricity regulator's report was made public, most electricity shares (including those of the rival) increased in value. The individual's acquittal appears to have occurred for several reasons. Amongst them were that, he had expressly sought the advice of his employer's company secretary before openly making the purchase in the rival; the secretary apparently did not believe the information was either unpublished and so not public (numerous letters had gone out) or price-sensitive, a view that was shared by the individual and the jury. Nevertheless, it seems that the question as to whether the information was sufficiently 'particular' that it was capable of going to a jury, albeit covering at least 12 companies, was answered in the affirmative by the trial judge.[35]

Specific or Precise

Under section 56(1)(b) inside information also has to be 'specific or precise'. Frequently, it will be obvious that this requirement has been met, as in: 'At 11 am on 31st October ABC PLC will publicly announce an offer of £5 a share for XYZ PLC as part of a takeover bid'. However, in other cases it might be much, much harder to identify the dividing line between this type of information and inherently vague reports. Such questions are likely to turn on what was said, in what circumstances, and (it seems) any information the recipient of the information had about their source's connections and line of work.

No definition was provided in the Statute for 'specific' and 'precise', apparently because the legislators concluded that it would be: '... difficult if not impossible to give an exhaustive definition of all the circumstances

---

35   *The Independent*, 4 December 1996.

that would be covered by one word or the other'.[36] Although the two words appear to overlap to a considerable degree (Article 7.1(a) MAR merely uses 'precise' for the regulatory wrong), this will not invariably be the case, which explains the disjunctive connection.

During the Committee Stage of the Bill that became the CJA 1993, a government Minister in the House of Commons gave as an example of imprecise, yet specific, information the case of a company director who says to someone over lunch 'Our results will be much better than the market expects or knows'. Had he put a figure to the results, it would also have been precise. By contrast, the same committee thought that if, on a walk to the office car-park, an analyst observed that a company chairman's car was extremely battered and asked him if he should not replace it, and received a response that the chairman would not buy a new car that year, this would be neither specific nor precise information in relation to the fortunes of his company. There could be many reasons for such a statement, other than poor performance of the company, such as the personal finances (or general abstemiousness) of the chairman.[37]

In the years immediately after the FSA started actively prosecuting insider dealing, trial judges were sometimes required to address their minds as to what these terms might mean in specific cases. In early 2009, in *R v Carlisle* (unreported but discussed by Sarah Clarke in *Insider Dealing*) His Honour Judge Wadsworth concluded that dealing on the basis of a 'bare tip' on a particular company, given by a trusted friend, without any further information being provided, was not sufficiently specific, let alone precise, to constitute the crime. He thought that this situation might even extend to a comment such as: 'I can't tell you why, but if I were you I would buy shares in Bloggins Limited next week'. In these circumstances, the judge felt that the dealer would be relying not on knowledge but on the trust he had in a friend.[38]

Rightly or wrongly, taken to its logical conclusion, Wadsworth's analysis

---

36 David Kirk, 'Enforcement of Criminal Sanctions for Market Abuse: Practicalities, Problem Solving and Pitfalls', 2016, p.314.

37 Barry Rider *et al*, *Market Abuse and Insider Dealing*, 2016, p.61.

38 Sarah Clarke in *Insider Dealing: Law and Practice*, 2013, pp.67–68.

would significantly limit the effect of the legislation with regard to many of those accused as 'secondary' insiders. Short of direct evidence of the words used to prompt their dealing, and these being fairly explicit as to why securities should be bought or sold, a significant number of prosecutions might become untenable.

For example, suppose Uncle A, a broker in The City, wishes to assist his niece, Miss B. He asks her to meet him in Boulogne for lunch. During the meal he suggests that she buy shares in Company C, without explaining why she should do this (he has inside information). As both A and B are in France, no offence is committed by A under section 52(2) (tipping or disclosing) because of the territorial requirements for those offences set out in section 62(2) of the 1993 Act. Miss B then returns to London and purchases £100,000 worth of shares in the company and a few days later sees them soar due to the unexpected public announcement of a takeover bid. She immediately closes her position. Her trade is detected as potentially suspicious and a STOR is filed. She is subsequently arrested and prosecuted by the FCA for a section 52(1) offence. At trial, her counsel makes a submission of no case to answer. If Wadsworth's analysis were accepted, it would probably have to succeed. Perhaps for this reason, his thinking has not been followed in subsequent trials.

Instead, it seems to have been accepted that sufficiently precise inside information *can* be conveyed without being made explicit. According to this analysis, a key factor might be whether the recipient of the tip knew that it came from someone who, if only from their position, was likely to be exposed to inside information. In these situations, as Sarah Clarke has noted, it may be that recourse could be had to the notion of an assertion by inference.[39] In the hypothetical illustration, if Miss B knew that Uncle A was in a position to receive inside information as part of his job, his comment *might* be construed as an implied statement that a price-sensitive event would be published the following week, one that would drive up the price of shares in the company. This could then be deemed specific enough.

In *R v Adam Buck* (2012) (unreported but again discussed by Sarah Clarke

---

39   Sarah Clarke, *Insider Dealing: Law and Practice*, 2013, p.69.

in *Insider Dealing*), the defendant sought to argue in a submission of 'no case to answer' that there was no evidence that any specific or precise information had been passed to him. Mr Justice Simon rejected this argument and noted that such information did not even have to be detailed when it came to matters such as price and timing: 'Nor need the information be fully articulated. Thus, if a lawyer, banker or accountant who is known to be involved in takeovers or mergers, tips a friend to buy shares in a particular company it may, depending on the circumstances, amount to giving specific information, although there may be no further detail'. The case went to the jury, which accepted Buck's vehement denial of any wrongdoing and (unanimously) acquitted him (there were numerous legitimate explanations for what had occurred).[40]

As first instance determinations none of these decisions are binding. Although Mr Justice Simon's interpretation of the law might be necessary if a fourth attempt at producing a statutory criminal offence is to be avoided given current prosecution policy, and it is, of course, the view of a High Court judge sitting in the Crown Court, it does not allow for the subtleties of much human interaction, something that appears to have weighed heavily with His Honour Judge Wadsworth.

Not Made Public

Under section 56(1)(c) the prosecution must prove that the relevant information (the information that prompted the deal) had 'not been made public' when the trade occurred. If it had, no substantive offence would be committed, even if the accused person did not appreciate that this was the case, and thought that he or she was insider dealing. It is theoretically *possible*, if highly unlikely, that in these circumstances an attempt to commit insider dealing (albeit that it was 'impossible' to achieve) might be charged under the principle in *R v Shivpuri* [1987] AC 1, on the basis that: '… if the facts were as that person believed them to be, the full offence would have been committed by him'.

The issue as to when information had or had not been made public was

---

40   Sarah Clarke, *Insider Dealing: Law and Practice*, 2013, pp.68–69.

described by the Government of the day as the single problem that had caused most concern to organizations consulted prior to the passage of the CJA 1993.[41] There was good reason for this. Essentially, this provision requires the prosecutor to prove a negative, beyond reasonable doubt, something that is inherently problematic (and correspondingly rare) in the criminal law. As Lord Chief Justice, Lord Woolf observed in *R v Lambert and Ors* [2000] EWCA Crim 3542, if the Crown had to prove that a defendant was *not* suffering from diminished responsibility: '… it would be very difficult for the prosecution to satisfy a jury of the negative'.

The only realistic alternative to such a provision would be for the legislation to contain a *defence* of the information having already been made public, albeit one that only had to be raised by the accused person satisfying an evidential (rather than legal) burden, before the prosecution had to disprove it beyond reasonable doubt. This would, at least, assist the Crown in focusing its searches, but would raise numerous other problems. In *practice*, this issue appears to have been dealt with fairly pragmatically by the courts, which have (again) sought to prevent the 'mischief' that the Statute aimed to remedy going unregulated.

It is important to note that an offence will still have been committed if the source of the information that prompted the trade has not been made public, even if unsourced gossip to the same effect has been circulating for some time. For example, suppose that it has been widely rumoured for several months that A PLC is considering a takeover bid for B PLC. C is aware of this. However, he only purchases shares in B PLC after receiving a secret message, from one of the directors of the company, that such a takeover will be publicly announced the following day. Despite his awareness of the earlier rumours, C is still an insider.[42]

Section 58(2) of the 1993 Act defines when something is deemed to have been 'made public', although (and vitally) its provisions are not exhaustive. It was a late addition to the Bill that became the CJA 1993 after concern was expressed at the lack of guidance on this issue in the original draft. Information will be public if it is published in accordance with the rules of

---

41   Brenda Hannigan, *Insider Dealing*, 1994, p.67.

42   Karen Anderson *et al*, *A Practitioner's Guide to the Law and Regulation of Market Abuse*, 2017, p.49.

a regulated market for the purpose of informing investors and their professional advisers; is contained in records open to inspection by the public; can be readily acquired by those likely to deal in relevant securities; (and) is derived from information which has been made public.

The first of these is relatively straightforward. Companies listed on a UK Stock Exchange are bound by the Listing Rules (LR) which are under the oversight of the UK Listing Authority (UKLA), which itself is part of the FCA (prior to which it was part of the FSA). As a result, they are required to comply with UK disclosure and transparency rules and so obliged to publish price-sensitive information to the market in a timely manner. This is usually done via the LSE's Regulatory News Service (RNS), which publishes most regulatory and non-regulatory information produced by UK companies and a significant proportion of that emanating from across the Atlantic. Hundreds of announcements are made every day and almost 300,000 in the course of a year. Many of them are price-sensitive. Such announcements are visible on over two million market terminals, databases, and financial websites across the world.[43] Other markets have their own equivalents of the RNS.

Ironically, but perhaps unsurprisingly, such bodies have themselves spawned insider dealing. In December 2000, two former employees of the LSE pleaded guilty to charges under section 52. The pair reportedly met when working in the LSE's companies' announcement office, which received price-sensitive information about listed companies before allegedly releasing it via the RNS. It was said they passed this information on, on two occasions, prior to it being released.[44]

Public records would extend to registers such as the companies' or patents' registers and also official publications such as the *Official Gazette*. Information readily acquired by those likely to deal is, by definition, likely also to have affected share prices already, and so is no longer inside information. Information derived from material that has been made public allows for the legitimate role of analysts who put pieces of publicly released information together to draw a larger picture, even if that picture has not itself been

---

43   http://www.londonstockexchange.com/exchange/news/market-news/market-news-home.html
44   *Daily Telegraph*, 12 December 2000.

publicly released.[45]

Perhaps more problematically, under section 58(3) information may still be treated as 'public', even though it can only be acquired by exercising diligence or expertise; it has been communicated to a section of the public and not to the public at large; it is communicated only on payment of a fee; it is only published outside the United Kingdom; or it can be acquired only by personal observation. With regard to the last factor, and for example, a parliamentary committee suggested that the fact that a factory chimney could be seen by a small number of locally-based passers-by belching smoke at night, suggesting that it was working overtime (and so flourishing), would not be inside information as a result of section 58(3)(c) if it prompted them to invest in its shares.[46]

Alternatively, can be considered the (hypothetical) situation in which a trader regularly frequents an Italian restaurant and notices that the chief executive of a small PLC appears to be having regular but rather furtive 'working lunches' in a discreet booth, with the CEO of a much larger but similar company. He guesses that a takeover is in the offing and invests heavily in the smaller company's shares, which soar when the takeover is made public. It seems that no offence is committed. Nor would an offence be committed if he informed others of his hunch and they invested accordingly. However, had the trader crept up on the booth and 'eavesdropped' on the conversation, overhearing what was about to happen from the two men, knowing it was inside information from an inside source, and then traded on that information, he would be committing a crime.[47]

It has been suggested that sub-sections 58(2) and (3), taken together, are so broad that, in practice, information will be outside the scope of the offence if it could be surmised from information published anywhere in the world.[48] A fundamental problem in this regard is that the CJA 1993 was largely drafted before the emergence of the Internet and other electronic forms of communication. There is now a great deal more financial

---

45   Barry Rider *et al*, *Market Abuse and Insider Dealing*, 2016, pp.65–66.

46   Ibid, p.67.

47   Ibid, p.76.

48   Brian McDonnell, *A Practitioner's Guide to Inside Information*, 2012, p.235.

information readily available than was previously the case, often in a very easily accessible but extremely ephemeral form. Market participants, who are constantly on the lookout for new information, can easily claim that they have seen it mentioned after stumbling on such a forum, even if it has (allegedly) long since disappeared.

Sarah Clarke (a former FCA lawyer) has noted that to discharge the burden of proving that such information has *not* been made public, the regulator often adduces evidence of market movements from about the time of the alleged insider dealing. This is done on the basis that if significant price-sensitive information was made public via the Internet it might be expected that others (as well as the defendant) would have seen it and invested or sold accordingly, creating a noticeable 'blip' in the share price. However, on its own this is unlikely to be enough. The material may only have been posted for a very short period of time.

Normally, Clarke notes, the regulator will also have to demonstrate to the court that it has conducted appropriate searches of publicly available material and not found anything. To do this, it seems that the FCA usually instructs a company that specialises in monitoring information about corporate events to conduct a search into what was publicly available at the relevant time. They normally do this using sophisticated electronic search engines that are able to examine the Internet and published print media for information. A witness from the company can then testify that exhaustive searches had failed to reveal any public mention of the relevant information when the insider traded.[49] David Kirk has suggested that the regulator frequently has to go to 'extraordinary lengths' to prove a negative in this manner. There will often be forensic argument about exactly how far back the prosecution should search to find out whether any related information had been published before the date of dealing.[50]

Essentially, such companies are saying, 'Although we looked very hard we didn't find it so it cannot ever have been there'. Such an approach is not entirely devoid of intellectual support. The American logician Irving Copi

---

[49] Sarah Clarke, *Insider Dealing: Law and Practice*, 2013, pp.79–82.

[50] David Kirk, 'Enforcement of Criminal Sanctions for Market Abuse: Practicalities, Problem Solving and Pitfalls', 2016, p.317.

noted that: 'In some circumstances it can be safely assumed that if a certain event had occurred, evidence of it could be discovered by qualified investigators. In such circumstances it is perfectly reasonable to take the absence of proof of its occurrence as positive proof of its non-occurrence'.[51] However, it still requires a degree of confidence in human perseverance, thoroughness, and the efficiency of electronic search systems that not everyone will share, especially when it involves material that was posted many years earlier, as will sometimes be the case given the frequent delay in insider prosecutions. Doubtless, defence counsel in such cases will often expose jurors to the aphorism 'absence of evidence is not evidence of absence'.

It *might* be argued that, once such evidence has been adduced, what lawyers term the 'tactical burden' could apply to the accused: *Arbroath v Northern Eastern Railway Co.* (1883) 11 QBD 440. This arises when enough evidence has been adduced to meet the burden of persuasion with regard to an issue in the trial, if it was to go to the jury without rebutting evidence being advanced. This might require the defendant to provide some cogent evidence of his or her own as to exactly when and where he or she came across a public source providing him with the alleged insider information.

Nevertheless, if the defendant does so by claiming that he found it on the Internet, there is a problem. Unlike print media, the Internet is essentially transitory and unreferenced. Information that was once posted on it can be irretrievably lost to even the best search engines and most diligent enquirers. Furthermore, postings on the Internet can be taken down very rapidly. It is not entirely implausible (and so beyond reasonable doubt) that insider, price-sensitive, information about a security could be put up and removed before more than one or two people had seen and acted to it, failing to create a 'blip' in the share price, and then (eventually) being irretrievably lost for ever.

Likely to have a significant effect on price

Under section 56(1)(d) the information has to be likely to have a 'significant' effect on the price of securities. In practice, this 'market impact' test

---

51   Irving Copi, *Introduction to Logic*, 1953, p.95.

is one of the most important aspects of the statutory definition, and of the four criteria set out in section 56(1). It is often the hardest to establish.[52] It is a matter of degree. As a result, Kern Alexander separated the significant amount of 'confidential information' that is generated within a company and available to its directors, employees, and advisers, that might have *some* (albeit very modest) effect on share prices (and even on decisions to trade in those securities) from 'inside information' that is extraordinary in nature and reasonably certain to have a substantial impact on market price. (In the modern era, when financial derivatives can leverage even very small share price movements, this is potentially problematic).

Interestingly, Timothy Blackstone *may* have raised this distinction (if only obliquely) as part of his defence to insider dealing in 2003 (see below), on the basis that it was (allegedly) widely known that the company for which he was providing financial PR had been set up as a vehicle specifically to take over small mutually-owned building societies, and that information that they were planning to do just that with respect to a particular small building society did not achieve insider status for the purchasing company (rather than the target) as a result. (Blackstone had made no attempt to disguise his share purchase).[53] During debates over the earlier (1980 and 1985) criminal Statutes governing insider dealing, Government Ministers acknowledged that the kind of knowledge they were concerned with involved important occurrences that would have a fairly major impact on a company's prospects.[54]

Although even illustrative authority on this issue is limited, in 2000, the prosecution failed to establish a *prima facie* case against a stockbroker for a section 52(2) insider dealing offence. In throwing out the case, it appears that His Honour Judge Byers ruled, *inter alia* (there were several other very important grounds for his decision), that the information concerned (a mooted company buyout of a rival), to which the stockbroker had been privy, was *not* sufficiently price-sensitive. The judge pointed-out that the proposed deal — which might well not have gone through at all — was not

---

52   Brian McDonnell, *A Practitioner's Guide to Inside Information*, 2012, p.232.

53   *The Guardian*, 23 January 2003.

54   Kern Alexander, *Insider Dealing and Market Abuse: The Financial Services and Markets Act 2000*, 2001, p.12.

finalised until many months after the alleged 'encouragement' was given to a client (the DTI did not suggest information was ever passed-on), who might easily have sold the shares long before its conclusion. (The actual order was withdrawn before going through). Furthermore, the company itself was not an ideal vehicle for insider dealing with regard to this type of transaction, its shares being extremely stable, something that was evidenced by their relatively static price *after* the acquisition was publicly announced and concluded.[55]

Despite this last point, it is vital to reiterate that the price-sensitivity of information is determined at the time the trade takes place, when it is unknown to the public, *not* in the light of subsequent events. It is necessary to make what Sarah Clarke has termed a 'real-time' judgment of this issue. Indeed, there may not be any 'subsequent events', making it a purely hypothetical determination, as was the case with one anticipated takeover in *Sanders*.[56] It is also important not to confuse what happened to the share price when an announcement was actually made with price-sensitivity at the time of the dealing. That the price did rise or fall significantly after the information was made public is indicative that the information was appropriately price-sensitive at the relevant time, especially if the insider deal occurred very shortly before the information was publicly revealed; however, it is not conclusive. By the time it was publicly announced, especially if there has been a lengthy delay between dealing and publication, other factors might mean that the actual price move is small or non-existent.

For example, suppose that a dealer purchased shares in response to inside information that would normally drive their price up significantly, but it was publicly revealed at the same time as unrelated but catastrophic news about the same company. Alternatively, the inside information might be made public just as the entire market collapsed due to general factors, as occurred on 'Black Wednesday' in 1987. The dealer would still have committed an offence.

Conversely, it is theoretically possible that information that was,

---

55 *Daily Telegraph*, 19 December 2000.

56 Barry Rider *et al, Market Abuse and Insider Dealing*, 2016, p.78 and p.69; Sarah Clarke, *Insider Dealing: Law and Practice*, 2013, p.84.

objectively, not price-sensitive (and so not 'inside') albeit 'confidential' when it was obtained and influenced a suspect's trading, could have had a significant effect when eventually released due to intervening events. For example, suppose an armaments trading company makes a major but routine purchase of munitions shortly before a war (unexpectedly) breaks out; the conflict then allows it to sell them all overnight at a very considerable (and not envisaged) premium, greatly boosting its share price. The original purchase may well not have been price-sensitive, even if it contributed very modestly to someone's decision to deal in the company's shares. Furthermore, very occasionally, a major increase in share price might occur after fairly mundane news is made public, simply because of the irrationality and gossip that sometimes takes hold of markets.[57]

Additionally, that a dealer thought that inside information was highly price-sensitive does not necessarily make it so. For example, suppose that a director of a new but publicly listed department store, who is personally of very strong monarchical leanings, learns that it is about to be awarded a royal warrant. He secretly invests in its shares minutes before this is announced, expecting them to soar. The news has no observable effect on share value and, it transpires, this is the normal pattern for businesses awarded such a warrant in the modern era. No substantive offence is committed (but query again the *Shivpuri* possibility concerning whether there may have been an attempt: see earlier in this chapter).

Most of those who deal regularly using inside information make the occasional loss on insider deals, especially given the presence of substantial transaction costs. In *R v Asif Nazir Butt* [2006] 2 Cr App R (S) 44, the total profits made by the co-accused from 19 transactions were put at £388,488, but they also sustained losses of £100,681 from the trading, producing a net gain of £287,807. Many others make only modest gains on some deals, as was the case with two of the three insider trades alleged against Neel Uberoi (see *Chapter 2*).

The Statute does not contain specific guidance on what constitutes a 'significant effect', even if calculated when the deal occurred. One expert

---

57   For example, see Mary Arden and Geoffrey Lane, *Rotaprint PLC: Investigation under Section 432 (2) and Section 442 of the Companies Act 1985*, 1991.

witness has defined it as being a: '... movement in the price of a security which is not accounted for by normal market movements'.[58] In a regulatory context, Article 7.4 MAR 2016 provides that information is likely to have a 'significant effect' on price if it is of a type that a 'reasonable investor would be likely to use as part of the basis of his or her investment decisions'. This 'reasonable investor' definition has also found favour in criminal cases of insider dealing in some Commonwealth jurisdictions and might be adopted by criminal courts in England and Wales. Others will prefer a more precise test based on a minimum potential movement as a percentage of share-price, and a figure of ten per cent has been mooted in several cases, although it is certainly not a firm rule.[59] This might occasion problems with so-called 'penny shares', where even very modest increases might occasion large changes as a percentage of value.

---

58   David Kirk, 'Enforcement of Criminal Sanctions for Market Abuse: Practicalities, Problem Solving and Pitfalls', 2016, p.312.

59   Barry Rider *et al*, *Market Abuse and Insider Dealing*, 2016, p.70.

CHAPTER 5

The Statutory Defences and Punishment

Introduction

The section 52 offences are subject to the four general defences contained in section 53 of the Criminal Justice Act 1993 as well as to the more technical and recondite special defences found in Schedule 1 to the 1993 Act. Like all defences, they only become relevant to the tribunal's verdict if the prosecution have succeeded in proving all of the essential elements of the offence indicted, beyond reasonable doubt. In many cases, a defendant who pleads 'not guilty' will not be relying on a statutory defence, but merely denying one or more elements of the crime. For example, did they have the alleged inside information? As Barry Rider has noted, this is usually the best way of avoiding liability under the Statute.[1] However, in other cases, the accused will admit that the essential elements of the offence have been made out but will be basing his or her 'not guilty' plea on one of the statutory defences.

Of course, it is possible to do both, and this has occurred on several occasions. For example, in early 2003, it seems that PR consultant Timothy Blackstone denied that the alleged inside information he had received was such (an essential element of the offence), and also argued that, in any event, he had purchased the shares that were the subject of the prosecution 'to support the company' rather than in response to that information, this

---

[1]   Barry Rider *et al, Market Abuse and Insider Dealing*, 2016, p.77.

being an intention that he had held for many days before receiving the news, but delayed until he had been formally taken on as a consultant (a possible defence).[2]

Even so, David Kirk (former Chief Criminal Counsel to the regulator) has noted that defences do not feature very regularly in insider dealing trials, largely because the FCA would not usually proceed where an accused person could obviously avail himself or herself of one of them.[3]

Section 53: The General Defences

The four general defences set out in sub-sections 53(1)(a)-(c) and 53(3)(a) are of much more widespread significance and importance than those contained in Schedule 1. The section provides that an individual is not guilty of insider dealing if he or she shows (disjunctively) that they: 1) did not expect the dealing to result in a profit attributable to the information in question being price-sensitive; or 2) believed on reasonable grounds that the information had been disclosed widely enough to ensure that none of those taking part in the dealing would be prejudiced by not having it; or 3) would have done what they did even if they had not had the relevant information. Under section 53(2)(a)-(c) the same defences (suitably adapted) extend to those who encourage another person to deal in securities and who is accused under section 52(2).

Under section 53(3) an individual is not guilty of insider dealing by virtue of a disclosure of information under section 52(3) if he or she shows that they did not expect the 'disclosee' to deal in securities as a result of the disclosure or, although he or she had such an expectation, did not expect the dealing to result in a profit attributable to the fact that the information was price-sensitive.

Defences and the Burden of Proof

To adopt the statutory terminology, the defences set out in sub-sections 53(1), (2) and (3) have to be 'shown' by the accused person. Using normal

---

2   *The Guardian*, 23 January 2003.

3   David Kirk, 'Enforcement of Criminal Sanctions for Market Abuse: Practicalities, Problem Solving and Pitfalls', 2016, p.318.

rules of interpretation, this means that a legal (rather than merely an evidential) burden is placed on the defendant to 'prove' the defence. It is not enough for the accused merely to 'raise' it by adducing some tangible evidence (as is the case with an evidential burden). As such, these provisions constitute a *prima facie* exception to the 'Golden Thread' of English law, famously identified by Lord Sankey in *Woolmington v DPP* [1935] AC 462 in which, as a general rule, the Crown always bears the burden of proof. If the prosecutor establishes all of the essential elements of one or more of the section 52 crimes, and the defendant cannot persuade the tribunal that one of the statutory defences applies, he or she will be convicted, even if the jury retain a significant doubt in their minds about whether or not the accused is covered by that defence.

This interpretation accords with that reached for the defences set out under the Company Securities (Insider Dealing) Act 1985, in what was a less clear-cut statutory provision, given that the reverse burden on the defendant was 'implied', rather than 'express', under the principles set out in *R v Edwards* [1975] QB 27. In *R v Cross* (1990) 91 Cr App R 115 the Court of Appeal concluded that once the prosecution had proved each of the ingredients of the offence set out in section 1 of the 1985 Act, the burden of proof shifted to the defendant to establish one of the defences contained in subsections 3(1)(a)-(c) of the Statute, if he of she wished to escape liability. However, as was reiterated in *Cross*, and like all legal burdens placed on defendants, those now set out under section 53 CJA 1993 only need to be proved to the civil standard, that is on the balance of probabilities (or 'more probable than not'), rather than beyond reasonable doubt: *R v Carr-Briant* [1943] 1 KB 607.

Impact of the Human Rights Act 1998

Nevertheless, in theory, and as with all reverse burdens since October 2000, placing a legal burden on a defendant can be challenged under the Human Rights Act (HRA) 1998, on the basis that it is not compatible with Article 6(2) of the European Convention on Human Rights (ECHR), because the defendant is thereby deprived of the presumption of innocence, under which: 'Everyone charged with a criminal offence shall be presumed innocent until proved guilty according to law'. If the court came to the conclusion that it was a violation of Article 6, section 3(1) of the HRA might be employed to circumvent the problem. This provides that: 'So far as it is possible to do so, primary legislation and subordinate legislation must be read and given effect in a way which is compatible with the Convention rights'. This option is clearly preferred by the appellate courts to the only alternative, a declaration of incompatibility under section 4 of the HRA, which leaves the law as it is until Parliament intervenes: *R v A (No 2)* [2002] 1 AC 45.

Using an artificial construction of the statutory words, the provisions could then be 'read down' to the status of evidential burdens. These would merely have to be 'raised' by the defendant, by adducing some tangible evidence (often his or her own testimony), deemed sufficient by the trial judge to make the defence 'live', just as is the case with general criminal defences, such as 'self defence': *R v Lobell* [1957] 1 QB 547. Case law suggests that this test, especially when placed on defendants, is not particularly demanding: *Jayasena v R* [1970] AC 618. This having been done, the prosecution would acquire an extra legal burden, in addition to those pertaining to establishing the essential elements of the offence, namely to disprove the relevant defence beyond reasonable doubt. It should be noted that evidential burdens are always deemed to be compatible with Article 6(2): *R v Director of Public Prosecutions, ex parte Kebilene* [2000] 2 AC 326.

Are the defences set out under the 1993 Act compatible with the ECHR? This is a difficult question. Although the right to a fair trial is absolute under the convention, the presumption of innocence is not. Case law indicates that some, but not all, reverse legal burdens *are* convention-compliant. The European Court of Human Right's attitude to reverse burdens was set out most fully in *Salabiaku v France* (1988) 13 EHRR 379, which noted that Article 6(2) requires States to: '… confine them within reasonable limits, which take into account the importance of what is at stake and maintain the rights of the accused person. This test turns on the circumstances of the individual case'. In deciding whether a *prima facie* infringement of Article 6(2) is 'proportionate', and so convention compliant, case law suggests that the courts consider a number of factors. These include, *inter alia*: the nature of the mischief that the provision is designed to combat (how serious a threat is it to the wider society); the essential elements of the offence that the prosecution have to prove before the burden is transferred to the accused (how narrow is the burden placed on him or her); the respective difficulty that the prosecution or defence would face if required to prove the matter in question; and the penalty for the offence if proved (is it essentially a 'regulatory' matter or is it a true 'crime' that carries serious punishment): *Sheldrake v DPP* [2005] 1 AC 264 and *R v DPP, Ex parte Kebilene* [2000] 2 AC 326.

Rather strangely, it appears that the Court of Appeal has not yet been asked to consider the issue of compliance with regard to any of the defences set out in section 53 CJA 1993, even though juries that have been directed that it places a legal burden on the accused have gone on to convict. Several informed observers feel that the legal burdens placed on defendants in insider dealing cases are 'proportionate' and so acceptable, not least because some of the factors normally considered by the courts when deciding convention compliance militate in favour of such an analysis.[4] Certainly, the defendant is best placed to prove, for example, that he or she would have dealt in the securities in any event, irrespective of the inside information (see below). It was partly for this reason that in *R v Lambert and Ors* [2000] EWCA Crim 3542 the Court of Appeal concluded that the burden placed on a defendant pleading the partial defence (to murder) of diminished responsibility did not violate Article 6(2).

Despite this, some observers are rather less sure about convention compliance. It has been noted that some of the defences set out in section 53 are not limited to straightforward questions of status or exemption but also involve concepts such as reasonableness and good faith. The possibility of the latter being present is sometimes construed in a defendant's favour when it comes to deciding on the proportionality of a reverse legal burden.[5]

Perhaps most importantly of all, the way insider crimes are viewed and punished has changed drastically since reverse burdens were first placed on defendants in the 1980s, when they were close to being quasi-regulatory offences, almost never producing custodial sentences. The increasingly heavy terms of imprisonment being imposed, and the growing social stigma

---

4   Sarah Clarke, *Insider Dealing: Law and Practice*, 2013, p.131.

5   Clare Montgomery *et al*, *Fraud: Criminal Law and Procedure*, 2015, at D.5.39.

occasioned by such convictions, might now argue in favour of them being evidential burdens. They increase the injustice of an erroneous conviction and, given that insider dealing is much less of a threat to the wider society than murder (to consider the *Lambert* situation), might produce a fundamentally different result when it comes to balancing community interests against those of the accused.[6] As a result, the possibility that an appellate challenge would be successful cannot be entirely excluded.

It should, of course, be noted that there are four different defences set out under section 53. The same factors will not necessarily apply to all of them in equal measure. It would certainly be possible for different decisions to be reached on convention compliance with regard to each one of them, as was the case with those in the Hunting Act 2004: *DPP v Anthony Wright* [2009] EWHC 105 (Admin). The four defences are briefly addressed below.

Section 53(1)(a)

Under section 53(1)(a) it is a defence that a person accused of insider dealing did not expect the trade to result in a profit attributable to the information in question being price-sensitive in relation to the securities concerned. Section 53(6) makes clear that this extends to not expecting to avoid a loss as well.

It is quite difficult to envisage situations in which this defence will operate. However, in Parliament, a Government Minister suggested that it might apply to someone who was in possession of inside information that was likely to drive up the price of a particular share that he held, when made public, but who then sold them before the information was released (rather than purchasing further shares), so missing what would otherwise be a potential gain.[7] The defence is only available to someone accused of dealing or encouraging another to deal, not a person accused of disclosing information.

Section 53(1)(b)

Section 53(1)(b) of the Act provides for a defence based on disclosure. It is a rarely used and rather technical provision by which an accused person will

---

6   David Hamer, 'The Presumption of Innocence and Reverse Burdens: A Balancing Act', 2007, p.146.

7   Sarah Clarke, *Insider Dealing: Law and Practice*, 2013, p.121.

not be guilty if he or she believed, on reasonable grounds, that the relevant information, although still 'inside' and not publicly available, had been disseminated 'widely enough' (a lower threshold than publicly available) amongst parties to a potential transaction for them not to be prejudiced by its absence. The defendant has to prove that there was no unfairness and so a level playing field for all of those involved. The government, when introducing this defence, suggested that it might be useful in underwriting transactions where both parties were aware of the relevant information so that neither was at a disadvantage, whatever the wider situation might have been with regard to such knowledge.[8]

Section 53(1)(c)

The defence set out in section 53(1)(c) is (arguably) the most important of the four. Under it, a defendant who is able to show that he or she would have traded in the relevant securities anyway, irrespective of the inside knowledge that he or she possessed, can avoid conviction. Interestingly, even in 1976, the City Company Law Committee had mooted that if insider dealing was criminalised there should be a defence premised on ignoring or disregarding inside information in the dealer's possession when trading, albeit noting that: 'In practice, a jury may seldom accept such a defence, but there may sometimes be contemporary evidence to support it'.[9]

Section 53(1)(c) covers several possible scenarios. Perhaps most obviously, it allows those dealing under some sort of severe financial compulsion to secure an acquittal, even though they are in possession of inside information when they trade. Thus, the defence might extend to a desperate and sudden need for cash to deal with a serious emergency. For example, A owns shares in B PLC, his or her only significant assets. He or she receives inside information about the shares which, when made public, will see their value fall precipitously. Very shortly afterwards, before the information has been made public, his or her uninsured spouse C falls gravely ill while on holiday abroad. C requires an immediate and very expensive operation and then to be flown back to the UK by air ambulance. A could liquidate his

---

8   Barry Rider *et al*, *Market Abuse and Insider Dealing*, 2016, p.79.

9   Anon, *Insider Dealing*, 1976, p.7.

or her shares in B PLC to fund the operation, benefiting from the higher price that they still fetch, and hope to rely on this provision to avoid liability for insider dealing.

More complex (and perhaps likely) scenarios in this regard present greater problems. For example, a rapidly failing small business urgently needs money to purchase machinery. The owner sells a tranche of shares in a blue chip company that he or she knows will fall when price-sensitive information is made public, before this happens, using the money to re-equip their own firm. Might the defence apply, and is it just a matter of degree?

However, the defence does not merely cover those who are compelled to deal. Thus, Barry Rider has suggested that a trustee who, while possessing inside information about shares, dealt in them after receiving independent advice, suggesting such a course of action, for the benefit of the trust, might also be able to rely on it.[10]

What of those who have evinced a settled intention to deal *before* they acquire inside information and then still go on to trade? Suppose that D is a fanatical follower of Liverchester Utd. He puts aside part of his earnings each month and makes a purchase of shares in the publicly-listed football club. He does this consistently, month in and month out, for two years before learning, as an insider, that an Australian tycoon plans to make a takeover bid that will drive the share price up. Even so, D continues with this normal monthly purchase, which takes place just before the share price increases. D might well argue that, as he or she had a provably settled intention to deal before becoming an insider, albeit that they completed the dealing afterwards, they are able to rely on the defence. Perhaps more realistically for this type of scenario, a company director may have agreed a share purchase or sale programme, running over a period of months or even years.[11] The issues would be exactly the same.

What of a man who has written to his broker (as the latter will confirm) stating that he or she is 'determined' to buy a tranche of shares in a certain equity but has not placed a formal order before becoming an insider? As

10   Barry Rider *et al*, *Market Abuse and Insider Dealing*, 2016, p.79.

11   David Kirk, 'Enforcement of Criminal Sanctions for Market Abuse: Practicalities, Problem Solving and Pitfalls', 2016, p.318.

the evidence of such a settled intention becomes smaller, it will of course become progressively much more hard for the defendant to discharge the legal burden placed on the issue, even on a balance of probabilities.

Section 53(2)(a)-(c)

Section 53(2) employs much the same wording as section 53(1) to provide the same defences in regard to those accused of encouraging others to deal in price affected securities contrary to section 52(2). For example, section 53(2)(a) and (c) are almost exact mirrors of section 52(1)(a) and (c). However, the wording in section 53(2)(b) suggests that the defence will also be available if the defendant can show, on reasonable grounds, that where he or she encouraged someone to deal in the future, they believed the information 'would be' sufficiently widely disclosed, by then, to prevent anyone involved in the dealing from being prejudiced. Barry Rider notes that this might apply to information that was in the course of coming out but had not yet fully done so, or that had been time embargoed.[12]

Section 53(3)

Section 52(2)(b), the disclosing offence, has its own special defences set out under section 53(3). Although there is no requirement for the Crown to prove causation as an essential part of its case, section 53(3)(a) provides that an individual is not guilty of insider dealing by virtue of a disclosure of information if he or she shows that they did not, at the time, expect any person to deal in securities because of the disclosure or, alternatively, under section 53(3)(b), shows that although they had such an expectation they did not expect the dealing to result in a profit attributable to the fact that the information was price-sensitive in relation to those securities. This represents a narrowing of the insider dealing offence when compared to the situation under the 1980 and 1985 Acts, where such a defence was not available.[13]

For an extreme (and unlikely) example of the section 53(3)(a) limb of the defence in operation can be considered the situation in which a company director, seeking spiritual guidance while on a religious retreat, mentions to

---

12   Barry Rider *et al*, *Market Abuse and Insider Dealing,* 2016, p.80.

13   Clare Montgomery *et al*, *Fraud: Criminal Law and Procedure,* 2015, at D.5.35–36.

an elderly Carthusian monk that his or her company was about to be taken over by a wealthy and larger rival. After their discussion, the monk, who had come into an inheritance that very morning, immediately climbed out of the Charterhouse and rushed up to London to invest in the company before its share price soared. (Of course, the monk would probably be guilty of an offence under section 52(1) of the same Statute).

Much more pertinently, juries might well accept that if a director tells his spouse something over dinner he or she could not reasonably expect that the other would use the information to trade in shares the following day. More generally, Barry Rider has suggested that unauthorised disclosures of inside information might be excused in situations where the insider believes, on reasonable grounds, that the recipients are highly honest professional people who are unlikely to break the law.[14]

The test contained in the second defence, set out in section 53(3)(b), is likely to be quite difficult to satisfy, once the Crown has established that the defendant was an insider who was aware that they had inside information, and it is rarely seen in practice.

The Schedule 1 Defences

Those who drafted the relevant provisions in the CJA 1993 were faced by the conflicting need to punish insider dealing while still permitting the financial markets to operate efficiently (they are a vital part of the British economy). During the debates on the Bill, Anthony Nelson MP, then Chief Secretary to the Treasury, observed: '… we must not inhibit unreasonably the legitimate practices and expertise of those in the City of London'.[15] The special defences in Schedule 1 are one of the fruits of this difficult endeavour, and designed to ensure that specialist financial practices that are legitimate, longstanding, and often vital to efficient market functioning are not criminalised. They are of very limited application and can be dealt with swiftly.

Schedule 1 divides these highly particularised defences into those pertaining to: 1) 'market makers', 2) 'market information' and 3) 'buy-back

---

14   Barry Rider *et al, Market Abuse and Insider Dealing*, 2016, p.80.

15   David Kirk, 'Enforcement of Criminal Sanctions for Market Abuse: Practicalities, Problem Solving and Pitfalls', 2016, p.313.

programmes and stabilisation'.[16] These defences apply only to dealing and encouraging type offences.

Market makers

This is a defence that protects the reasonable activities of market makers. A 'market maker' is a person who holds themself out at all normal times in compliance with the rules of a regulated market or an approved organization as willing to acquire or dispose of securities; and is recognised as doing so under those rules. This defence exists to protect the defendant who can demonstrate that they were acting in good faith in the course of their employment or business, for example, by entering into an agreement for the underwriting of an issue of financial instruments.[17]

Market information

It is also a defence for someone to show that their actions were in connection with the facilitation of the acquisition or disposal of securities, and that the information they had as an insider was market information arising directly from their involvement in the acquisition or disposal.

Buy-back programmes and stabilisation

Essentially, this defence allows dealing in inside information in order to maintain the market price of the security in question. The nature of the defence means that the circumstances in which dealing of this kind is permissible are necessarily limited. Those engaging in stabilisation and buy-back programmes should notify the FCA.[18]

The Punishment of Insider Dealing

Insider dealing contrary to section 52 CJA 1993 is an 'either way' offence, meaning it can be tried summarily before magistrates or on indictment in the Crown Court depending on 'mode of trial' procedures and the accused's right to elect trial by jury in any event, albeit that cases of summary trial are

---

16   Criminal Justice Act 1993, Insider Dealing Provisions, Slaughter and May, April 2006.

17   An example from the regulatory regime is provided in MAR 1.3.7 G.

18   stabilisation@fca.org.uk.

almost unheard of. In theory, it could even be dealt with by a formal caution administered by the police at the behest of the FCA, in lieu of prosecution. On summary conviction, the defendant would be liable to a fine not exceeding £5,000 and/or imprisonment for a term not exceeding six months or, if two or more charges produce consecutive sentences, a maximum of a year.

Much more significantly, under section 61 of the CJA 1993, insider dealing is punishable by a maximum sentence of seven years imprisonment and/or an unlimited fine if sentenced in the Crown Court. The former has never come close to being imposed, with the four-and-a-half years given to Martyn Dodgson in 2016 being the current maximum, although, in *R v Asif Nazir Butt* [2006] 2 Cr App R (S) 44, a sentence of five years' imprisonment was initially passed, before being reduced to four by the Court of Appeal. Its initial length was influenced by the defendant, it was said, having committed a gross breach of trust in his position as the compliance officer of an investment bank, but was reduced on appeal because the judge failed to give proper weight to the 'guilty' plea (always an important factor given the expense of proving such cases). In 2012, after pleading guilty to ten counts of insider dealing, James Sanders also received four years' imprisonment, and it seems that the four to five year bracket is currently the tariff for those who are prominently (rather than peripherally) involved in most 'serious' cases.

The sentencing powers open to UK courts exceed the minimum sentencing standards set out in the EU Directive on Criminal Sanctions for Market Abuse of 2014 (CSMAD), although the UK (like Denmark) is not a signatory to this agreement, and does not intend to implement it.[19] Even so, the government has publicly announced that the country's criminal sanctions regime for market abuse will be at least as strong as that contained in CSMAD. In June 2015, the *Fair and Effective Markets Review* (FEMR), established by the Chancellor of the Exchequer the previous year to help restore confidence in the way financial markets operate, and conducted by the FCA, the Bank of England and the Treasury, went further, and suggested that the maximum possible penalty be increased to ten years. In part, this was because seven years was lower than that available for other economic

---

19   2014/57/EU.

crimes, such as fraud, bribery, or money laundering, despite being comparable to them in the potential harm caused. It was also felt that although no criminal insider dealing case had yet been heard that involved all potentially aggravating factors at the same time, such cases might occur in future, possibly warranting more than the existing maximum, particularly if there had been a very severe breach of trust or sophisticated criminality by organized groups.[20]

By some international comparison, the maximum *potential* sentence for insider dealing is relatively mild in the UK. Up to 20 years' imprisonment can be imposed for the offence in the USA and South Korea, and the longest sentences passed in America, although well short of this, have exceeded those in the UK by a large margin. For example, Raj Rajaratnam received eleven years' imprisonment for insider trading in 2011 and Matthew Kluger a sentence of 12 years in the same year. It should be noted that five other countries and territories have a maximum prison term of ten years for the crime: Canada, Australia, India, Hong Kong and China (other than Hong Kong).[21] Against this, the proportion of insider-trading defendants in the UK who receive custodial sentences (around half), although behind Australia, is ahead of Ontario (Canada), Hong Kong, and the USA. Even more significantly, the *average* length of custodial sentences in these countries and territories is fairly similar, with the USA and Australia being slightly ahead of the UK and Hong Kong a little behind.[22]

In *R v McQuoid* [2010] 1 Cr App R (S) 43 the Court of Appeal gave detailed guidance on the considerations that might be relevant to sentencing in insider dealing cases, and particularly the 'aggravating' and 'mitigating' factors which apply to the offence and the offender. (Most are fairly predictable and found in many other white-collar crimes). The former include: any breach of trust; deliberate, planned and dishonest action; a high level of sophistication; any steps taken to conceal criminal conduct; offences committed over a prolonged period involving a large number of individual

---

20   *Fair and Effective Markets Review: Final Report*, 2015, pp.88–89.

21   James H. Thompson, 'A Global Comparison of Insider Trading Regulations', 2013, pp.1–23.

22   Lev Bromberg *et al*, 'The Extent and Intensity of Insider Trading Enforcement—An International Comparison', 2017, p.18.

trades; high levels of profit made; acting in a group; and the impact of the offence on overall public confidence in the integrity of the financial markets. They also endorsed earlier comments by Mr Justice Hughes (as he then was) that professional City traders might expect more draconian punishment.[23]

This guidance has been supplemented on a piecemeal basis by subsequent judicial decisions. For example, genuine remorse, suffering extreme financial consequences as a result of such a conviction, and delays in bringing the matter to trial have all been viewed as mitigating factors, but not that it involved selling shares to avoid a loss rather than buying them to make a profit. In 2013, after sentencing Richard Joseph to four years' imprisonment (concurrently) on each of six counts of conspiracy to deal as an insider, His Honour Judge Pegden expressly observed that an element of deterrence was needed when sentencing such cases, not least because this type of behaviour is inherently difficult to detect and prove. Joseph had made almost £600,000 from insider dealing, in shares such as those of the brewer and pub retailer Greene King, material manufacturer Fiberweb, and engineering firm IMI, but had paid his inside source almost £200,000 for the information.[24]

Even so, several more recent defendants have received much more lenient disposals than some of these 'headline grabbing' cases might suggest, if not as mild as the punishments that were usually imposed for the offence during the first 20 or so years after criminalisation. This is especially likely where: there have been guilty pleas (which seem to produce a significantly larger discount than with many other crimes, whatever the theory); the sums involved have not been enormous; it was a 'one off' trade; the perpetrators were not employed in the finance industry; those accused were peripherally involved; or there has been co-operation with the FCA.

For example, Manjeet Singh Mohal and his neighbour Reshim Birk pleaded guilty in the first week of their jury trial (not at the earliest opportunity) in November 2016. Birk, who was said to have made about £100,000 from dealing in Logica shares after a tip-off from Mohal, was sentenced to 16 months, suspended for two years, and 200 hours of community service. Mohal received a ten months' sentence suspended for two years and 180

---

23   *Fair and Effective Markets Review: Final Report*, 2015, p.89.

24   *Daily Telegraph*, 11 March 2013.

hours of community service. Judge Nicholas Cooke QC said he did not impose a custodial sentence because the middle-aged men were of previous good character, although this (like their age profile) is common in insider dealing cases. He also took into account the delay since the offending in 2012 although, again, this is not particularly uncommon in such cases: 'These are men of previous clean character; one made no benefit that can be proved. Those who commit financial crime can be hit in the pocket and given community work, even when it crosses the custodial threshold'. However, he also noted that Birk was a 'lucky man' not to be facing prison.[25]

In 2015, a former senior executive, was slightly less fortunate after he pleaded guilty to insider dealing in shares, after learning of his employer's impending partnership with the company (a breach of trust), as a result of which he had made a profit of £79,000. Even so, he was sentenced to just one year in prison.[26] Mark Lyttleton received the same disposal in 2016, despite being a senior figure in the finance industry, after he pleaded guilty to two counts of insider trading that had taken place during his time at Blackrock some years earlier. Unusually, he had voluntarily paid an undisclosed financial penalty rather than going through confiscation proceedings in the courts. His apparent remorse and co-operation, and the relatively modest profit made (£35,000) contributed to the court's leniency.[27]

Those who are convicted of insider dealing offences might also find themselves subject to action under the Proceeds of Crime Act 2002 (POCA). The relevant powers include confiscation orders requiring payment to the State of any benefit obtained by the commission of a crime. For example, in a case brought by the FCA, and heard at Southwark Crown Court between 10 and 15 September 2014, confiscation orders totalling £3,249,488 were made against the five men who had been convicted of insider dealing during trials held in 2012 and 2013 in connection with 'Operation Saturn'. In this case, the total amount confiscated exceeded the profits generated by the crimes because the confiscation regime allows the court, in appropriate circumstances, to assume that profits from other trading (to that charged), that

---

25   *Financial Times*, 13 January 2017.

26   *Daily Telegraph*, 3 March 2015.

27   *Daily Mail*, 21 December 2016; see also FCA Press Release, 21 December 2016..

took place within the same period, also represent the proceeds of crime.[28] In April 2015, one of the five, Pardip Saini was sentenced to a further 528 days imprisonment (on top of his original sentence) for failing to pay £222,047.46 of the £464,564.91 confiscation order made against him the previous September by the designated date of 12 March 2015.[29] This is quite normal with confiscation orders. In 2012, after their convictions for insider dealing, Christian and Angie Littlewood were ordered to pay £767,000 each or face another three years' imprisonment.[30] It is certainly a more effective way to enforce such an order than the civil debt procedure used for unpaid fines imposed under the regulatory procedure.

To facilitate the recovery of such money, under section 40 of POCA, a restraint order over 'realisable property' can be obtained as soon as a criminal investigation has begun (even before a defendant's arrest) so as to prevent the dissipation or concealment of assets that are likely to be seized after a conviction. Furthermore, a substantial prosecution costs order might be awarded against those convicted of insider dealing, perhaps unsurprisingly, given the complexity of the cases involved. For example, in 2016, both defendants, Manjeet Mohal and Reshim Birk, were ordered to pay £42,000 each in costs. Mark Lyttleton was ordered to pay the FCA £83,225.62, despite his early guilty plea.[31]

The FCA's RDC can also ban those *convicted* in a criminal court from conducting regulated activity using its powers under section 56 FSMA 2000 (a 'prohibition order'), just as it can those who are dealt with via the regulatory route. Thus, a year after receiving two years' imprisonment for insider dealing Damian Clarke was reportedly also given a lifetime ban by the regulator, on the basis that he was not a fit and proper person to perform 'any function in relation to any regulated activity carried on by any authorised person'. (In theory, such a ban could be appealed to the tribunal, within 28 days of the subject receiving the Final Notice containing it). In this case, the notice expressly cited the aggravating features identified by the

---

28   FCA Press Release, 15 September 2014.

29   FCA Press Release, 28 April 2015; *Ft Adviser*, 28 April 2015.

30   *The Independent*, 20 August 2012.

31   FCA Press Release, 21 December 2016.

trial judge in the criminal case to explain the length of the ban imposed.[32]

---

32   FCA Final Notice to Damian Frank Clarke, Reference Number: DFC01043, 1 June 2017.

CHAPTER 6

Evidential Perspectives

Introduction

The evidential test for bringing a criminal prosecution (discussed in *Chapters 2–4*) is not easily satisfied in insider cases and actually securing a conviction is, of course, even harder. This chapter highlights a number of issues that are particularly significant in, or relevant to, insider dealing trials, several of which help to explain the difficulty involved in bringing such cases while others suggest why some trials still result in convictions, despite these problems.

Nature of the Hearings

Some of the difficulties faced by the regulator when prosecuting insider cases are structural, and apply to many other sophisticated forms of white-collar crime. As Margaret Cole noted in 2007: 'The transactions are often complex and not jury friendly'.[1] The offences are highly technical and often occur against a background of complicated financial markets. Jurors may be faced with lengthy trials, and large amounts of evidence. A month is usually the minimum duration for the simplest contested hearings of this type and, in 2016, the main trial flowing from the 'Operation Tabernula' investigation (see below) lasted over 12 weeks (still shorter than the trial in 'Operation Saturn' four years earlier). In a rather plaintive note to the judge prior to his

---

1   Speech by Margaret Cole to American Bar Association, 4 October 2007.

majority direction in this case, the jury stated that: 'After nearly two weeks and looking at the evidence very carefully, we may be reaching an impasse'.[2]

In these circumstances, what may be clear to financial services professionals, such as stockbrokers, city solicitors and accountants, can easily become confusing or obscure to laymen, even if they are assisted by the extensive use of graphics, interactive exhibits, and PowerPoint slides, as often occurs in the modern era. (Southwark Crown Court, which is currently used for all insider hearings, is well equipped for this purpose). A jury that cannot fully understand the evidence is very unlikely to feel that it has been persuaded beyond reasonable doubt of the prosecution case.[3] It may be for this reason that a prosecution barrister recently noted, after a major insider dealing trial, that: 'If you are defending, you want to make it as complicated as possible'.[4]

Expert Evidence

Linked to the above, and a notable feature of insider dealing cases, is that much of the jurors' understanding is necessarily dependent on what they can learn from expert testimony. The prosecution usually has to call expert witnesses to give opinion evidence on vital matters, such as the price-sensitivity of the alleged inside information, and the defence frequently do the same to rebut this testimony.[5]

Among those called have been market analysts from prominent firms of stockbrokers, academics in relevant fields, senior bankers, and even those with expertise in the oil and gas industry (which was germane to a particular case). They often play a crucial role, sometimes being required to give opinion evidence on purely *hypothetical* situations, such as: 'In my opinion, if this takeover bid *had* been revealed when the defendant dealt, although it did not subsequently go ahead, it would have had a very significant effect on X PLC's share price'. There are also often considerable presentational

---

2   *Financial Times*, 6 May 2016.

3   Margaret Cole, 'Insider Dealing in the City'. Talk at the London School of Economics, delivered on 17 March 2007.

4   Aleksandra Jordanoska, 'Case Management in Complex Fraud Trials: Actors and Strategies in Achieving Procedural Efficiency', 2017, p.347.

5   David Kirk, 'Enforcement of Criminal Sanctions for Market Abuse: Practicalities, Problem Solving and Pitfalls', 2016, p.315.

difficulties in putting this type of opinion evidence before the jury.[6]

As in other trials, both criminal and civil, such witnesses can be challenged as to their expert status or whether the issue before the court warrants expert opinion evidence: essentially, do the jury need expert assistance and can the tendered witness provide it? It is for the judge to decide these questions. The former will only rarely pose difficulties. Unlike, for example, routine anxiety and mental distress, the average jury member is not familiar with financial markets or practices and so needs help: *R v Turner* [1975] 1 QB 834 and *R v Hayes* [2015] EWCA Crim 1944.

However, whether a tendered witness is sufficiently skilled or knowledgeable to give an expert opinion can be more problematic. English courts take a relatively generous approach to granting expert status, but there are limits to their broadmindedness, and situations in which such status has been refused: *R v Inch* (1989) 91 Cr App R 51. As is well known, expert status can be achieved by professional experience: *R v Awoyemi and Others* [2016] EWCA Crim 668. Nevertheless, most tendered experts in insider cases have an array of professional qualifications, and membership of professional bodies that are relevant to the finance industry, as well as extensive personal experience of work in financial services.

Finding a suitable expert in what is a highly specialist field can be extremely difficult, for all parties.[7] In 2000, after the DTI insider dealing prosecution of a former vice-chairman of a leading stockbrokers was thrown out on a submission of 'no case to answer', it was reported that the trial judge had criticised the prosecution's expert witness, the compliance director from another leading stockbrokers, who (allegedly) had no personal broking experience and kept no notes of the conversations he had held after he 'relied on and sought opinions of others'. (Experts are treated more liberally than other witnesses when it comes to the use of hearsay that forms part of the corpus of knowledge in their specialist field).[8] When cross-examined on specific details, the expert (apparently) accepted almost every proposition

---

6   Ibid, p.318.

7   Ibid, p.318.

8   See *R v Abadom* (1983) 1 All E.R. 849 and s.118(1)(8) CJA 2003.

put to him by defence counsel.[9] Interestingly, it was reported that a second expert witness who was tendered by the prosecution in the same case was not ultimately heard after his impartiality was questioned.[10]

The career of Dr Thomas Walford, who gave expert assistance in the insider dealing trials emanating from Operations Saturn (2012) and Tabernula (2016), is illustrative of a well-qualified and experienced expert witness in such matters. In 2016 he was one of very few experts who publicly offered to provide opinion evidence and assistance in insider dealing cases (whether regulatory or criminal), being registered with Expert Evidence International Ltd. Dr Walford had spent 19 years managing private banks and nearly 30 years in The Square Mile managing or advising clients on their investment and banking needs, as well as being certified as an expert by the Expert Witness Institute. He was also, *inter alia*, accredited by the: UK Register of Expert Witnesses; the Expert Witness Institute; the Academy of Experts; CEDR (conflict management and resolution consultancy); and was also a member of the Chartered Institute of Arbitrators.[11] Professor Paul Barnes has also provided expert evidence and assistance in several high-level insider cases (and numerous other financial crime trials). He had a distinguished academic career as Professor of Finance and Fraud Risk Management at Nottingham Business School in the UK and in other universities, is a qualified Chartered Certified Accountant, an academic member of the Association of Certified Fraud Examiners, and the author of numerous books and articles in the field.[12]

Even if experts can be found it is sometimes difficult to get them to testify firmly on inherently difficult issues such as price-sensitivity (particularly if it is hypothetical), even though this might be a crucial aspect of the case.[13] Like all experts, those in insider dealing cases owe their first duty to the court, not to the party calling them. They must make the court aware of any limitations on their evidence or expertise, any areas in dispute that are outside

9   *Daily Telegraph*, 19 December 2000.

10 *The Guardian*, 19 December 2000.

11 expert-evidence.com

12 www.paulbarnes.org.uk

13 Margaret Cole, 'Insider Dealing in the City'. Talk at the London School of Economics, delivered on 17 March 2007.

their competence, and any change in their opinion: CPR 2015, Rule 19.2.

Absence of Intercept Evidence

The SEC and other American law enforcement agencies have made extensive use of undercover investigative techniques in insider-dealing cases, where it has frequently played a crucial role in prosecutions. This has often extended to the use of 'intercept evidence'. Historically, British law enforcement agencies have had less experience than their counterparts across the Atlantic in this regard. However, in recent years this has changed, to some extent, and such techniques are increasingly employed in England and Wales. The Regulation of Investigatory Powers Act 2000 (RIPA) currently governs the covert interception of private communications, whether made via telephone, post, text or email, by police or intelligence agencies. The best known of these is a telephone 'tap', albeit that the rise of new technologies means that there are numerous others.

As a relevant public body for the purposes of sections 28–29 of RIPA, there is no institutional barrier to the FCA employing surveillance techniques (it is one of many agencies so empowered) and in recent years they have done so extensively. Such interception requires authorisation from the Home Secretary, who must consider it necessary and proportionate on one of a small number of grounds, including the prevention or detection of crime (the most likely to be advanced for insider dealing) under section 28(3)(b) of RIPA, before he or she issues a warrant. A Code of Practice provides additional guidance on when and how the powers under RIPA should be used.

Nevertheless, one reason that UK agencies have less experience than their American counterparts in insider cases is the limited use that can be made of such material in the UK, and this continues to be the case. In almost all common law jurisdictions 'intercept evidence', that is recordings or transcripts made from intercepted communications, is admissible at trial. For example, when federal prosecutors in America charged one man and his firm, a hedge fund, with insider trading in 2011, the trial was notable for the use of wiretap evidence that had been collected from telephone calls made between the six defendants and others, all of whom were unaware that their calls were being recorded. This included the man telling a subordinate to create an email chain that would suggest they had discussed investing in a particular stock for legitimate reasons, to hide the fact that his interest had actually been sparked by an inside tip.[14]

However, section 17(1)(a) RIPA (effectively) prevents the use of intercept evidence obtained 'at any place in the United Kingdom' in UK courts, whether civil or criminal. It does this by providing that no such evidence shall be adduced or referred to that in any way discloses its origin or the circumstances in which it was obtained. The government has traditionally justified this by claiming that intercept material is more valuable as intelligence rather than as evidence against suspects. If intercepted communications were used as evidence, it would make suspected criminals aware of the methods used by the police to acquire it. This would lead to suspects adopting counter-measures to avoid interception. Additionally, it is feared that it would lead to a heavy administrative burden on the prosecution as, for the use of intercept evidence to be consistent with a fair trial, all relevant intercepted material collected during the course of an investigation would have to be retained and catalogued so that it could be made available to the defence (including unused material in the hands of the prosecution).

Rightly or wrongly, intercept evidence is used only as a source of intelligence in the UK, although this may change in the future. Ironically, intercept evidence obtained abroad by a foreign police agency might be admissible in a criminal trial in England and Wales, unless excluded under PACE, and this is certainly not automatic: *R v James Lee* [2015] EWCA Crim 851.

Nevertheless, intercept evidence must be distinguished from evidence obtained by other forms of covert surveillance, such as recordings made using hidden listening devices or 'bugs' to eavesdrop on suspected criminals, which *are* admissible in criminal proceedings, even where they record a telephone call taking place (albeit that they might only record one side of it). Thus, in *R v E* [2004] EWCA Crim 1243, evidence of recordings of the defendant talking on a mobile phone while in his car made by a secretly planted surveillance device were held to be admissible as it was not an interception for the purpose of RIPA 2000: 'What was being recorded was

---

14   Jonathan Barnard, 'Insider Trading: An Easy Offence to Commit', 2011, p.15.

not the transmission but the words of the accused taken from the sound waves in the car'. It had the same status as conversations with passengers (also recorded by the bug).

Of course, in these situations an application might still be made under section 78 PACE to exclude the evidence on a discretionary basis. Even so, it will not necessarily be successful: *R v Roberts (Stephen Paul)* [1997] 1 Cr App R 217. In *R v Khan (Sultan)* [1997] AC 558, the House of Lords upheld a decision that evidence obtained by a bugging device, attached by the police to a private house without the knowledge of its owner or occupiers, was admissible and should not have been excluded under section 78 PACE. The crime being investigated (major Class A drug-dealing) was very serious, justifying the invasion of privacy (also a *prima facie* violation of Article 8 ECHR) and its attendant trespass and damage. As was noted by the Court of Appeal in *R v King* [2012] EWCA Crim 805, evidence obtained through the use of covert audio equipment: '… is admissible and any infringement of a suspect's Article 8 rights will not automatically result in the exclusion of the evidence so obtained'. Of course, the gravity of insider dealing is not usually on a par with high level drug-dealing, unless huge in scale, which will come into consideration, reducing the justification for such drastic action. Against this, the intrusion into the suspect's privacy has often been slightly more modest in insider cases, with offices rather than homes being bugged, etc.

Furthermore, RIPA has no effect on the recorded phone calls and emails of employees, that have been preserved by a firm, which are still, of course, admissible, as would have been the situation in the *Sanders* case had the defendants not pleaded guilty (see below). The availability of such recorded material is not a new phenomenon. In the insider dealing case of *R v Gray and Others* [1995] Crim LR 45, brought under the 1985 Act, much of the prosecution evidence was in the form of telephone conversations between the appellants which had, as a matter of routine, been tape-recorded by their employers and obtained by a Department of Trade and Industry (DTI) inquiry.

It is now mandatory to record such calls, increasing their potential availability. Since March 2008, the regulator's *Conduct of Business Sourcebook*

(COBS) has required that all regulated firms record telephone conversations and electronic communications (including emails, instant messaging and faxes) relating to transactions made on their premises, and retain such records for at least six months. Furthermore, they must be held in a medium that is readily accessible by the FCA, where any corrections or other amendments (and their contents prior to such changes) can easily be ascertained, while it must not be possible for the records to be otherwise manipulated or altered.[15] The FCA initially applied an exemption to recording conversations on mobile phones and other handheld devices at work, but since November 2011 these must be recorded as well. The FCA's retention requirements will increase in 2018, after which records of conversations will be stored for a minimum of five years (rather than six months). In practice, little will change. Even in the 'noughties' it seems that most City investment banks kept these recordings for at least five years, in large part to prevent insider dealing.[16]

Serious Organized Crime and Police Act 2005

In 2007 Margaret Cole observed that England could not match the American ability to plea bargain in insider cases, something that: '... without a doubt, enables more effective prosecutions in front of juries'.[17] Certainly, the SEC Enforcement Division's co-operation programme has been highly effective. It will often enter agreements with admitted insider dealers and grant them leniency in exchange for testifying against others, so providing vital testimonial evidence where it would otherwise be lacking.

However, the difference between the USA and England and Wales has decreased markedly in this regard since the extensive powers contained in sections 71 to 75 of the Serious Organized Crime and Police Act 2005 (SOCPA) came into force (in April 2006) and the FSA was then granted powers as a 'specified prosecutor' to enter into agreements under the Statute, a power still held by the FCA. The regulator is now able, and quite willing, to offer major inducements to encourage those involved in insider dealing

---

15   FCA, *Conduct of Business Sourcebook*, 01/04/2013, para 11.8.10.

16   Geraint Anderson, *Cityboy: Beer and Loathing in the Square Mile*, 2009, p.136.

17   Margaret Cole, 'Insider Dealing in the City'. Talk at the London School of Economics, delivered on 17 March 2007.

to make full admissions (usually a prerequisite for any agreement), assist the prosecution, incriminate others, and give evidence for the Crown. In part, this is probably because their employment in such situations does not raise the popular anxiety that it would with some other (more conventional) crimes. However, for both prosecutor and defendant, such a procedure has attendant risks: *R v Hayes* [2015] EWCA Crim 1944. It is also a very complicated matter, with delicate 'scoping interviews' being required prior to decisions being made.

Sentence Reduction

Under section 73(1) and (2) of the 2005 Act, where a defendant has pleaded guilty and, pursuant to a written agreement made with a specified official, offered to assist the investigator or prosecutor, the Crown Court (it is purely a matter for the judge) can pass a significantly reduced sentence, one that is commensurate with the 'extent and nature of the assistance given or offered'. This might make the difference between immediate custody and a non-custodial disposal, especially where the sentence would not have been more than a year's imprisonment. (It will not occur automatically with longer periods of imprisonment, even for white-collar criminals: *R v Dougall* [2010] EWCA 1048).

This was the situation in one of the FSA's first 'plea bargaining' cases using SOCPA powers, in 2011, after a former trader pleaded guilty to insider trading as part of an arrangement with the FSA, and was sentenced to ten months' imprisonment suspended for two years, and 300 hours of community service. The trial judge, Geoffrey Rivlin QC, told him that it was only the: '… quite exceptional mitigating factors such as the swift and timely admissions to the FSA and other matters such as the SOCPA agreement that saves you from immediate imprisonment today'.[18] The trader agreed to give evidence against another man, who had placed spread-bets in numerous listed companies using the information he (the trader) had provided, and who was convicted of 22 counts of insider dealing and sentenced to two years' imprisonment.[19] In this case, the man's solicitor had approached the

---

18   *Daily Telegraph*, 22 June 2010.
19   *Daily Telegraph*, 15 December 2011.

FSA and indicated a willingness to co-operate a month after the FSA and City of London Police had executed search warrants on addresses associated with the two men. Discussions were then conducted leading to the plea and co-operation agreement, although, it seems, he was not ultimately called to give evidence.[20] Similarly, in 2013, when an accused pleaded guilty and agreed to provide assistance in exchange for a more lenient disposal he, too, received a suspended (rather than immediate) prison sentence.[21]

Immunity

In the case involving Malcolm Calvert (referred to at various other places in this book), the far more radical (and rarely used) provisions set out under section 71(1) of SOCPA were employed. These provide that if a specified prosecutor thinks that, for the purposes of the investigation or prosecution of an offence, it is appropriate to offer someone immunity from prosecution he or she may give the person a written 'immunity notice'. The Attorney-General must first be consulted by designated prosecutors in such cases, and consent to such a drastic course of action, before any decision is made on granting full immunity. Under section 71(2) of the Statute no proceedings for the specified offence can then be brought against that person unless, and crucially, he or she fails to comply with any conditions specified in the notice: section 71(3). Usually, the condition is giving evidence for the prosecution. In the Calvert case such an agreement was reached between the FSA and a witness, who avoided criminal charges for insider dealing by helping to prosecute the defendant. Instead, the FSA fined him the £59,098 he had profited from, using its civil regulatory powers (without even the addition of a punitive element to the fine). By the time of trial, this witness was suffering from a serious illness and was unable to give evidence in person;nevertheless, a statement he had made was read to the jury as admissible hearsay, pursuant to section 116(2)(b) CJA 2003, on the basis that its maker was unfit to be a witness because of his bodily or mental condition. When making the application to read this statement out to the jury, the prosecution candidly declared that, without it, the case against Calvert was not sufficiently

---

20   Sarah Clarke, *Insider Dealing: Law and Practice*, 2013, p.256 and p.89.
21   *Financial Times*, 19 May 2016.

strong to found a realistic prospect of conviction.[22] It should be noted that a conviction based decisively on evidence adduced from an absent witness (as was the case in *Calvert*) does not automatically amount to a breach of the ECHR: *R v Horncastle and Others* [2009] UKSC 14. Everything turns on the facts of the case and the proper application of evidential safeguards.

To a significant (if not total) degree, the FSA's arrangement with the witness in the Calvert case (above) does resemble the aggressive system of plea bargaining found in the USA. Of course, this has considerable dangers. Prior to 1994, there would have been a mandatory accomplice corroboration warning to the jury as to the dangers of convicting on such evidence (abolished by section 32 of the Criminal Justice and Public Order Act 1994). Even today, although there is no legal requirement for a warning, there would normally be some form of discretionary judicial direction on its risks: *R v Makanjuola* [1995] 1 WLR 1348. Anecdotal evidence—section 8(1) of the Contempt of Court Act 1981 precludes formal studies on this issue—suggests that jurors often dislike such evidence, perceiving it to be unfair, and are sometimes reluctant to convict on it without firm supporting material. Whether the Crown would always feel able to justify such a benign approach, even in insider cases, is also debatable.

Good Character of Defendants

As with many white-collar crimes, the profiles of those accused of insider dealing are often very different to those of 'typical' defendants in the Crown Court, something that complicates the prosecution's task and adds to the jury's problems. Given that the majority of the defendants in insider dealing cases work in finance, most will be without previous convictions of any type, and so are what the Court of Appeal described in *R v Hunter and Others* [2015] EWCA Crim as being of 'absolute good character'. (The court also reiterated that this status did not require positively creditable acts, such as helping the underprivileged). As Lord Judge noted in *McQuoid*: '... it will often be the case that it is the individual of good character who has been trusted with [inside] information just because he or she is an individual of

---

22   Sarah Clarke, *Insider Dealing: Law and Practice*, 2013, p.256.

good character'.

As a result, if accused of a crime, they will be entitled to the full double-limbed direction set out in *R v Vye* [1993] 3 All ER 241 as to its effect on both their credibility when giving evidence, *if* they elect to testify (the first limb) and their propensity to offend (the second limb). Essentially, they will be, very obliquely, told that it makes them less likely to have committed the crime before the court and more likely to be telling the truth. As Lord Steyn observed in *R v Aziz* [1996] 1 Cr App R (S.) 265, the '... good character of a defendant is logically relevant to his credibility and to the likelihood that he would commit the offence in question'. Of course, not all insider-dealing defendants give evidence at trial. Some exercise their right not to go into the witness box, and so are only entitled to the propensity limb in *Vye*, even if they risk having an adverse inference direction given to the jury under section 35 of the Criminal Justice and Public Order Act as a result.[23] Nevertheless, most do testify at trial.

In *Hunter* the Court of Appeal slightly narrowed the circumstances in which a good character direction should be given, feeling that these had sometimes been 'extended too far' and convictions quashed in surprising circumstances. Even so, it is unlikely that, for example, a previous conviction for drink-driving, as was the case with one insider dealing defendant, would deprive the accused of at least most of the benefits of a (suitably modified) good character direction. In these situations the trial judge might direct the jury that the defendant had 'no relevant convictions' and should be treated as a person of previous good character before going on to give a suitably modified *Vye* direction. As many defendants in this type of case will also be, to some degree, middle-aged or even elderly, this will be particularly significant. The accused person will have reached mature years without offending, something that may well weigh heavily with jurors.

Suspicious Behaviour

An important feature of many insider-dealing trials can be found in the generally 'suspicious' behaviour of convicted defendants. This is often absolutely

---

23   The jury must be warned about the limitations on the adverse inferences they can draw.

vital in building the prosecution case and rendering the finer points of the complicated provisions found in Part V CJA 1993, especially the essential elements of section 52 and its attendant section 53 defences (*Chapter 4* and *Chapter 5*), of marginal relevance. Where an accused person has gone to considerable lengths to disguise or hide his or her dealing, as is frequently the situation, it is difficult for them to argue that their conduct was outside the terms of section 52. If he or she really thought that that was the case, why would they try to conceal it? If the inside information came from a legitimate source, why then trade (by way of illustration) under an unknowing partner's name or through an acquaintance or chain of acquaintances? Similarly, why hide the records of alleged insider transactions? For example, Martyn Dodgson and another man used unregistered mobile phones, encoded and encrypted records, safety deposit boxes, and payments in cash, something that did not help their cases at trial.[24] In like manner, once Mark Lyttleton breached Blackrock's policy requiring him to declare all personal trading accounts held by his immediate family, by keeping just one of them back, and two mobile phones were recovered from his house (one of them unregistered and the other registered to a fictitious name and address), both of which contained a single contact number with a foreign asset manager, he was not ideally placed to resist a criminal prosecution.[25] By contrast, cases where defendants traded entirely normally, in their own names, have sometimes produced acquittals.

Circumstantial Evidence

One of the biggest problems facing prosecutors in insider dealing cases lies in the quality of the evidence that is usually available; most importantly, much of it is circumstantial. In 2007, Margaret Cole argued that there is rarely a 'smoking gun' in insider dealing investigations. In the majority of cases, she suggested, the prosecution is unable to obtain direct evidence that a person knowingly possessed and used inside information. As a result: '… virtually all insider trading cases hinge on circumstantial evidence'. According to Cole, the best that prosecutors in insider dealing cases can normally do is

---

24   FCA Press Release, 12 May 2016, updated 30 November 2016.

25   *FT Adviser,* 22 December 2016.

to invite the jury to infer proof from such *general* matters as: the fortuitous-ness of the timing; the size of the share purchase; the fact that the defendant had never traded in a particular stock or even market sector before. Cole went on to suggest that, at the most, there might be some provable contact with a person who may have been in a position to pass-on price-sensitive information. This last might be termed *specific* circumstantial evidence and appears to be accorded a different status by the regulator.[26]

In *practice*, it seems that general circumstantial evidence that relates purely to the fortuitousness of a deal (both the selection of shares and its timing), or even several deals, which is totally uncorroborated by anything more, has never been prosecuted to conviction by a jury, and rarely if ever prosecuted at all. This situation is certainly not unique to the UK, being found in most other Anglophone jury-utilising countries, such as Canada.[27]

For example, suppose a private investor has never previously dealt in equities. He or she suddenly invests heavily in an obscure share, just before the announcement of good news, their value soars, and he or she closes their position. When questioned, they simply maintain that they 'felt like a flutter' and selected this share at random by sticking a pin in the financial pages of a newspaper, and 'got lucky'. Would the coincidence be enough to found a criminal conviction? The answer is almost certainly 'no'. These things do, sometimes, happen. More surprisingly, suppose he or she makes just six share purchases between 1st January and 31st December the same year (a period when the market has been fairly stable). Each one precedes a takeover bid or similar event that drives the share price up, resulting in a significant profit on all of the trades. They are interviewed by the FCA and merely say, again, that they chose them at random. Experience suggests that it is still very unlikely that he or she would be indicted for insider dealing, let alone found guilty although, statistically, such things almost *never* happen.

The FSA/FCA appears to proceed on the basis that even a significant number of highly suspicious trades are not enough, *per se*, to justify criminal

---

26 Margaret Cole, 'Insider Dealing in the City'. Talk at the London School of Economics, deliv-ered on 17 March 2007.

27 Hongming Cheng, *A Comparison of Illegal Insider Trading in Canada and Post-Communist China*, Simon Fraser University PhD. Thesis, 2004, p.155.

prosecution, without establishing at least a provable link to an insider. Arguably, this can be seen from their initial treatment of Helmy Omar Sa'aid, a London juice bar owner and the principal dealer in the Littlewood case (see below). An examination of Sa'aid's transaction record found that he had traded just prior to 22 merger or acquisition announcements between 2000 and 2008. Even so, on its own, this was not thought sufficiently damning to go to a jury. It was first felt necessary to identify a firm link to an identifiable insider in the relevant deals, which the FSA ultimately succeeded in doing when they traced his connection to investment banker Christian Littlewood and his wife Angie.[28]

Similarly, in Operation Saturn the very prescient deals originating with the Mustafa brothers had been noticed some months before formal action was taken, which only occurred after a text from one of the brothers to a dealer was detected (although Ali Mustafa was convicted, his brother Erin Mustafa remains it seems on the NCA's most wanted list).[29] More recently, a team from the FSA and the Serious Organized Crime Agency (now the National Crime Agency) spent a year tracking a suspected insider-trading ring as part of Operation Tabernula (see below), after receiving suspicious transaction reports about their share dealings. Formal action was only taken after they positively identified a potential source for the traders' information.

Circumstantial evidence is traditionally contrasted with 'direct' evidence. The latter is unmediated proof of a fact in issue, such as eye-witness testimony of a crime. The former is indirect evidence, that is, it is proof of one or more facts from which the tribunal can find another fact established. It is largely based on the drawing of inferences, via inductive reasoning, to prove the suspect's guilt. It is not necessarily 'inferior' evidence. It has been said that circumstantial evidence is capable of proving a proposition with the accuracy of mathematics: *R v Taylor, Weaver and Donovan* (1928) 21 Cr App 20. By contrast, some direct evidence, such as that of visual identification in difficult circumstances, is notoriously unreliable. Nevertheless, circumstantial evidence has some inherent dangers, which can weigh heavily with juries, especially in insider dealing cases.

---

28   *The Guardian*, 5 February 2011.

29   http://www.nationalcrimeagency.gov.uk/most-wanted-hub/item/36-ersin-mustafa

Although the conclusion reached via deductive argument is certain, that produced by inductive reasoning is merely probable. Its premises suggest some degree of support for a conclusion, but do not necessarily lead to it. The Scottish judge and legal scholar David Hume (nephew of the famous philosopher of the same name) noted that: '... in any case of pure circumstantial evidence, it is always possible the prisoner may be innocent, though all the witnesses have sworn to nothing but the truth; a thing which cannot happen, where they swear directly to a deed as done in their own presence'.[30]

In insider cases, the general circumstantial evidence normally adduced as indicative of dealing is usually consistent with other possibilities, such as an exceptional run of good luck, market acumen, or, where a number of shares have increased in price over a relatively short period of time, stocks rising in a bull market. As a result, tribunals would be required to make an assessment of probability before convicting on such evidence. In this situation the courts' traditional nervousness about employing statistical probability theory and mathematical models (for all types of evidence), and the expert evidence that grounds them, when assessing evidential cogency, probably explains the FCA's reluctance to rely on *purely* circumstantial evidence of dealing patterns. Without the use of probability theory such evidence is of very limited value.

Rejection of mathematical models

Anxiety about the use of mathematical models in a forensic environment is longstanding and can be seen in the Court of Appeal's criticism of the employment of Bayes' theorem (which calculates the odds of one event happening given those of other related events) in relation to DNA evidence in the 1990s: *R v Adams* [1998] 1 Cr App R 377. More recently, in *R v T* [2011] 1 Cr App Rep 85, the defendant's appeal against his conviction for murder was allowed after the Court of Appeal held that, when it came to evidence of shoe-marks, no attempt should be made by forensic scientists to use mathematical formulae such as likelihood ratios to calculate the probability of finding a matching shoeprint, where firm statistical evidence did not exist.

---

30   David Hume, *Commentaries on the Law of Scotland, Respecting Trial for Crimes*, 1797, Vol. II, p.385.

It should be noted that this nervousness is not unique to either the UK or to criminal tribunals. For example, and famously, Harry Markopolos's mathematical assessment of Bernard Madoff's returns, and his conclusion that they could only have been obtained by fraud (a huge Ponzi scheme as it transpired), on the basis that no money manager could have such consistent and uniform month-to-month success, was repeatedly made (and ignored) for almost a decade before Madoff was finally exposed.[31]

It seems that there is an innate degree of concern about such assessments because they cannot be readily understood by laymen and because of fears that the probabilistic reasoning itself might be wrong even though it has the verisimilitude of scientific reliability. Certainly, numerous mistakes in causal reasoning and erroneous generalisations using statistics have been identified over the years.[32] Amongst them have been the problems occasioned by the employment of statistics in 'shaken baby syndrome' cases during the first decade of the current century: *R v Clark* [2003] EWCA Crim 1020.

Perhaps unsurprisingly, given the much lower standard of proof found in civil cases, it seems that purely circumstantial evidence, even of a fairly general type, *is* sufficient to produce a finding against a defendant accused in the RDC and (by extension) presumably the Upper Tribunal as well, whether under the MAR or its predecessor in FSMA. For example, in 2008, an IT support engineer employed by Body Shop, was found by the committee to have hacked into the company's computers and then 'shorted' its shares using 'contracts for difference', just before an unexpected profits warning was issued in January 2006, despite the absence of any direct evidence to this effect. The engineer made a profit of £38,000 on the CFD trade (He came to the FSA's attention after one of his brokers filed an STR). The case against him boiled down to a combination of: opportunity, coincidence, and his willingness to take a very significant financial risk.

The support engineer's position meant that he had access to senior executives' passwords, including those of the CEO and the company's chairman, allowing him to read confidential emails if he so wished, although there

---

31 *The Guardian*, 24 March 2010.

32 See generally, C Wang, *Sense and Nonsense of Statistical Inference*, Marcel Deker Inc., New York, 1993.

was no direct evidence that he had ever done so. He reportedly borrowed £29,000, more than his annual salary, to deal. Although he had some previous record in spread-betting, it had been more modest in scale, and of a slightly different nature. Against this, he *had* traded two CFDs in Body Shop on earlier occasions and adamantly denied the allegation, stating that he made the bet purely as a result of his own research and assessments. For example, he had concluded that Body Shop shares were overpriced in early January 2006 because their P/E ratio was one of the highest in the UK retail sector at 20 after rising rapidly over the previous year. Furthermore, shortly before trading, at the end of the Christmas period, he had spent a day working at the chain's Brighton store, where his (quite legitimate) personal observation suggested that things were not going well for the company.

The FSA relied purely on the circumstantial case against him. Significantly, in its Final Notice to the support engineer, the RDC acknowledged that it was unable to demonstrate 'conclusively' that he had had access to inside information at the Body Shop. Arguably, this was a tacit admission that the case could not have reached the criminal standard of proof had it been brought in such a forum (assuming, purely for the purposes of argument, that all of the vital prerequisites for such an action were made out). Even so, the committee felt that the matter had been established and fined him £85,000.[33] The engineer initially referred the case to the Upper Tribunal but (most unfortunately for legal observers) did not pursue the matter.

Cost

Investigating and prosecuting all but the simplest cases of insider dealing, especially those committed by sophisticated perpetrators, is notoriously slow and resource intensive. Inevitably, this has an impact on whether prosecutions are brought. A reluctance to spend such money partly explains the modest level of pre-2008 prosecutions and why some potentially criminal but 'hard to prove' cases are still abandoned today. Cases can take years to complete, if only because of the huge number of documents that have to be found, scrutinised, and in some cases prepared for trial. When it came

---

33   FSA Final Notice, 1 July 2008; Barry Rider *et al*, *Market Abuse and Insider Dealing*, 2016, p.90; *The Times*, 2 July 2008.

to Operation Tabernula, the figures were astounding. The whole eight-and-a-half years investigation cost nearly £14m and, at its height, involved 40 full-time staff, with a permanent core of ten to 12 people. The electronic documents examined required 10.5 terabytes of storage space. The FSA/FCA also drafted in the National Crime Agency (formerly SOCA) to assist with obtaining phone records and putting suspects under covert surveillance. They gained access to and scrutinised 120 different telephones (30 of them unregistered) and SIM cards; examined 35,000 calls between City brokers; and made 485 requests for telephone traffic details (which number called which number, etc.). They also had recourse to cell site analysis to estimate whether, when, and where the suspects met, and considered telecoms data from Spain, Dubai and the USA that had been produced as the suspects travelled around the world. A bug planted in an office was monitored in real time for several months. Some 46 lever arch files of statements were produced.[34]

Perhaps fortunately, the FSA/FCA's enforcement division's budget has grown substantially over the past decade. In the year ending 31st March 2013 it was £65.2 million, raised by charging fees to authorised firms carrying out regulated activities (the FCA is not a publicly-funded prosecutor, unlike the SFO).[35] Nevertheless, it is not unlimited, and some theoretically prosecutable cases will be abandoned because the investment needed to make them viable is simply deemed to be too great.

---

34 *The Guardian*, 12 May 2016.

35 https://www.fca.org.uk/about/the-fca; See also Jonathan Fisher, *Who Should Prosecute Fraud, Corruption and Financial Markets Crime?*, 2013, p.2.

CHAPTER 7

FSA/FCA Prosecutions

Introduction

The Department of Trade and Industry (DTI) and the Serious Fraud Office (SFO) normally prosecuted insider dealing during the first 15 years after the advent of the Criminal Justice Act 1993.[1] (Very occasionally, the City of London Police and the Crown Prosecution Service also became involved in prosecuting such cases).[2] For example, in early 2003, the DTI prosecuted a small scale insider dealer to conviction (by a majority verdict) in 2003. He was fined a nominal £1,000. It was a relatively minor case in terms of monetary value in which he had made less than £3,500, having traded, in his own name, in a company by which he had been briefed as a PR consultant about an imminent takeover.[3] On a much larger scale, in 2004, four members of an Essex-based insider dealing ring were prosecuted by the SFO, convicted, and sentenced to imprisonment (the longest term being 30 months). The ring used information provided by the proof-reader in a local high-security printing firm that specialised in producing confidential documents who, while working night shifts, saw commercially sensitive material, including

---

1   The Criminal Justice Act 1987 established the Serious Fraud Office and gave it power to conduct any criminal proceedings that appeared to relate to serious or complex fraud.

2   David Kirk, 'Enforcement of Criminal Sanctions for Market Abuse: Practicalities, Problem Solving and Pitfalls', 2016, p.319.

3   *The Guardian*, 23 January 2003. See also *The Times Briefing*, 23 Jan 2003.

takeover proposals, before they were released to the Stock Exchange. He did not invest himself but was paid for information that he passed on to a woman and her business partner, who did purchase shares. The woman also passed on the tips to her estranged husband. The ring targeted 27 corporate deals between 1997 and 2001, such as Kwik Save's merger with Somerfield. Unlike the other three defendants, the husband pleaded 'not guilty' but the jury rejected his claim that he did not know that the share tips from his wife were based on insider knowledge.[4] Two years later, in an unrelated case, six men were prosecuted by the SFO for conspiracy to commit insider dealing.[5]

Advent of the FSA

In 2000, the newly created FSA was granted statutory powers under section 402(1)(a) FSMA to investigate and prosecute the offences set out in section 52 of the CJA 1993. These powers became operative in December 2001. (By contrast, the Securities Exchange Commission (SEC) in America cannot bring such prosecutions in its own right). For administrative convenience, the FSA was also given the power to prosecute other offences that were closely linked to the cases of insider dealing being charged, such as laundering the proceeds of such crimes, and this power has been upheld by the Supreme Court: *R v Rollins* [2010] UKSC 39.

The FSA has now been abolished and, for these purposes, replaced by the FCA, established by the Financial Services Act 2012, which came into force on 1 April 2013. The FCA is an independent non-governmental body financed by the financial services firms it regulates. It is accountable to the UK Treasury and Parliament and responsible for maintaining the integrity of the UK's financial markets. It has a wide range of investigative and enforcement powers, some of them equivalent to those held by the police and other special bodies such as HM Revenue & Customs. These include the power to apply for a warrant to enter premises for the purposes of search and seizure and the power to interview suspects under caution. It should be stressed that the exercise of these powers is not limited to those individuals or financial firms that the FCA regulates, but extends to anyone

---

4   *The Guardian*, 5 June 2004.

5   *R v Asif Nazir Butt* [2006] 2 Cr App R (S) 44.

who participates in the financial markets, even if they have no professional involvement with them, such as a purely amateur investor. The regulator has agreed a framework for liaison and co-operation in cases where another authority, such as the CPS or SFO, also has an interest in prosecuting any aspect of a case in which the regulator is also involved.[6]

Despite having held the statutory power to prosecute insider dealing for seven years, the FSA had never done so prior to 2008. Instead, it concentrated on its post-2000 regulatory powers for dealing with market abuse, meaning that the few criminal prosecutions brought during those years were instigated by other agencies. This is not entirely surprising. The FSA had many responsibilities, and did not then view itself as an enforcement-led regulator. It was also widely felt that such offences were simply too complicated for juries to understand, and excessively expensive to indict. Even after the CJA 1993 was passed into law, informed observers argued that the experience of the previous 14 years suggested that, despite the then Government's philosophical commitment to the primacy of penal sanctions, the criminal law was an unsuitable tool for dealing with all but a few cases of insider dealing.[7] Indeed, there was a strong body of thought that questioned the appropriateness of criminal sanctions for any such cases, and which suggested that it might amount to using a sledgehammer to 'crush a marshmallow'.[8] There was an almost general consensus that no jurisdictions, anywhere in the developed world, had achieved much success when trying to utilise the criminal law to deal with abusive activity in their capital markets, because the normal (and necessary) procedures and protections for defendants found in most criminal justice systems presented almost insurmountable barriers to the prosecution of such misconduct.[9]

Against this, others thought that the paucity of insider dealing prosecutions and convictions in the UK was troubling because the City of London

---

6   FCA *The Enforcement Guide* 01/04/2014, at para 12.11.

7   Keith Wotherspoon, 'Insider Dealing: The New Law: Part V of the Criminal Justice Act 1993', 1994, p.433.

8   Sarah Wilson, *The Origins of Modern Financial Crime: Historical foundations and current problems in Britain*, 2014, p.34.

9   Gary Wilson and Sarah Wilson, 'The FSA, "Credible Deterrence", and Criminal Enforcement—A "Haphazard Pursuit"?', 2014, p.12.

was home to one of the biggest stock markets in the world. Certainly, the FSA fared poorly in this regard when compared to enforcement authorities in some other European countries at this time. For example, in Germany, prosecutors obtained 36 convictions for insider dealing between 2004 and early-2010; in France, there were 12 convictions between 2004 and 2007; in Switzerland there were nine between 2004 and 2006, and even in The Netherlands, which has a comparatively small financial market, eight were secured in the six years after 2004.[10] Of course, Roman law countries, where the tribunal of fact is normally made up of professional judges rather than lay jurors, have some advantages when it comes to the prosecution of complex, white-collar crimes, as Lord Roskill's Independent Fraud Trials Committee of 1986, which proposed that major fraud cases be tried by a tribunal consisting of a judge and two specialist laymen, would probably have agreed.

A Change in Approach

A drastic change in approach to the use of criminal proceedings took place a few years after the advent of Margaret Cole to the position of Director of Enforcement of the FSA in 2005. However, it was not a purely personal effect. Even as the financial crisis was starting, in late-2007, it seems that the FSA made a conscious decision that its Markets and Enforcement Division would give a degree of precedence to prosecuting insider dealers under the CJA 1993 over pursuing them via the regulatory regime.[11] Such change was encouraged by criticism suggesting that the FSA's previous 'light-touch' style of regulation had been exposed as inadequate by the depths that the financial crisis reached in 2008, which was something of a turning point in attitudes towards this type of crime in much of the Western World. Officials also became concerned that perceived financial wrongdoing in The Square Mile might damage London's traditionally high standing as a major financial centre. As a result, there was considerable pressure, if not an element of straightforward compulsion, behind the decision to attempt to reduce such offences by enhancing 'credible deterrence' via criminal prosecution.

---

10   Jonathan Fisher, *Fighting Fraud and Financial Crime*, 2010, p.10.

11   David Kirk, 'Enforcement of Criminal Sanctions for Market Abuse: Practicalities, Problem Solving and Pitfalls', 2016, p.318.

There was, of course, an irony in this change in direction, occurring as it did just eight years after the limits on criminal actions for this sort of offence had been tacitly recognised by the introduction of the regulatory regime.[12]

It should be noted that the trend towards increased criminal prosecutions in insider cases since the financial crash is certainly not unique to the UK, being found in many parts of the developed world. For example, according to the Australian Securities and Investment Commission (ASIC), between 2011 and 2017, 35 people were criminally prosecuted in that country for insider trading as a result of ASIC investigations, with a conviction rate of over 85 per cent.[13]

Shortly after the financial crisis, a rash of prosecutions for insider dealing commenced, as a regime of largely civil sanctions, employed between 2002 and 2008, was replaced by a 'combined' civil and criminal approach, with the latter aspect now clearly in the ascendancy. Accompanying this development, and in response to critics who had suggested that a rapid staff turnover had resulted in insufficient financial expertise being accrued by the FSA's Enforcement and Financial Crime Division (EFCD), more and better qualified investigators and lawyers were appointed, especially to the FSA's criminal prosecution team, and improved computer systems developed to identify suspicious trading.

The FCA is now recognised as the lead investigator and prosecutor for insider dealing, although there is nothing, in theory, to prevent the CPS or SFO from bringing such actions (the DTI was abolished in 2007). Indeed, there is no inherent reason why section 6(1) of the Prosecution of Offences Act 1985, which allows individuals and companies to bring private prosecutions, should not be invoked in insider cases by, for example, financial firms, although this has never occurred.

It should be noted that the FCA is not unique in having such a role in specialist prosecutions. The Environment Agency (EA), the Health and Safety Executive (HSE), the Medicines and Healthcare Products Regulatory Agency (MHRA), the Department for Environment, Food and Rural

---

12   Gary Wilson and Sarah Wilson, 'The FSA, "Credible Deterrence" and Criminal Enforcement—A "Haphazard Pursuit"?', 2014, p.16.

13   Shirley Quo, 'The Moral Ambiguity of Insider Trading as a White-collar Crime', 2017, p.204.

Affairs (DEFRA), and several other bodies can all bring prosecutions in their own right. Some have argued for the creation of a single 'Financial Crimes Enforcement Agency' combining the SFO, FCA and other (similar) agencies, and so pooling expertise.

The FSA's change in approach towards pursuing criminal prosecutions after 2008 was sufficiently sudden that Christopher McQuoid, the first person convicted under the 'new' regime, raised it as a ground of appeal against his sentence of eight months' imprisonment. Rejecting this argument, and noting that some earlier suspects had been 'fortunate', the Lord Chief Justice, Lord Judge, observed that: 'If there ever was a feeling that insider dealing was a matter to be covered [purely] by regulation, that impression should be rapidly dissipated.'[14] In the ensuing years the FSA/FCA manifested a marked increase in its willingness to bring criminal prosecutions.

Typical Prosecutions

Although the substantive law on insider dealing is highly complicated—perhaps because of it—a majority of prosecuted cases still revolve around a fairly limited number of factual disputes, most of which are not legally complex. As Margaret Cole noted in 2007, experience suggested that the: '... difficulties in insider dealing prosecutions lie in establishing that someone did indeed possess inside information, establishing that the person knew it was inside information, and then traded on that basis'.[15]

This has always been the situation. An old case from Scotland, prosecuted under the 1985 Act, is illustrative of the primacy of factual rather than legal disputes in most insider trials. In 1991, an analyst for an Edinburgh stockbroker suggested to other employees of his company (i.e. brokers) that their clients sell some (not all) of their shares in a waste disposal and construction company. He gave this advice after holding a private, and wide-ranging, one-hour conversation with the company's chairman that was carried out in his professional capacity. At the ensuing criminal trial, the chairman insisted that he had specifically told the analyst that a profits

---

14   *R v Christopher McQuoid* [2009] EWCA Crim 1301.

15   Margaret Cole, 'Insider Dealing in the City'. Talk at the London School of Economics, delivered on 17 March 2007.

warning would have to be issued by the waste disposal company because of a downturn in the company's fortunes. There was no dispute that, for the purposes of section 10 of the 1985 Act, this would have been confidential, price-sensitive, information that the analyst would not have been entitled to divulge or (more relevant to the case) act on by telling other employees of his company to reduce their clients' holdings in the company's shares.

By contrast, the analyst was equally adamant that he had not been told anything about a profits warning, and had merely got the general impression that it would not be a particularly vintage year for the waste disposal company. It was accepted that for the purposes of the 1985 Act this would not be inside information and he would be entitled to (indirectly) advise his company's clients to trim their exposure as a result. About 1.9 million shares worth £5.7m were ultimately sold for £1,396,642 more than they would have fetched had they been sold after the profits warning was issued. The analyst was convicted by a majority verdict and fined, but the decision was quashed on appeal because the trial judge had mistakenly identified potential corroboration for the chairman's evidence (a requirement in Scottish law). The sole issue of importance was whether the appellant had been told about the profits warning by the chairman; the law, and its application to the case, was not in dispute.[16]

Most prosecutions do not involve defendants who say, for example: 'I saw speculation about this takeover bid on the internet several hours before I purchased shares in the relevant company and several days before that takeover was announced on the RNS; prove beyond reasonable doubt that I didn't if you can'. Nor do they involve accused persons who argue: 'This information was never likely to have anything other than the most modest, if any, effect on share price; any increase was just a co-incidence, occasioned by a generally rising market; it is up to you prove the contrary so that the jury are sure of my guilt'. Prosecuted cases normally involve defendants who say that they had never heard of the alleged inside information when they dealt, or who deny that they dealt at all.

To some extent, this state of affairs probably reflects reluctance on the part

---

16   *The Independent*, 17 February 1994.

of the regulator to bring criminal prosecutions in 'marginal' cases where there might be the possibility of a serious dispute about legal definitions. However, frequently, and perhaps not always wisely, there is often little dispute by the accused that the information involved was (for example) 'price-sensitive' or had not been made public. In part, this is because defendants who deny that they were aware of, or traded on the basis of, the alleged inside information sometimes feel that tactical imperatives preclude them from vigorously challenging whether the other essential elements of the offence have been made out. It can be difficult to say persuasively to a jury, at the same time, that the defendant did not trade using the relevant information and, in any event, even if he or she had, it did not meet all the definitional requirements of the CJA 1993, although the two positions are (logically) entirely compatible. The latter assertion might be deemed to hint at a lack of confidence in the former, effectively requiring defence counsel to say: 'He or she was not aware of this information, and if they were they could not have known it would have a significant impact on share price'.

This is important, as there is a general rule, albeit no longer a very rigid one, that a cross-examining party should challenge the evidence of an opposing witness on any issue to which they testify if he or she does not accept it ('putting the case'): *Browne v Dunn* (1894) 6 R. 67. A failure to do this may lead the trial judge tacitly to encourage jurors to accept unchallenged issues as proved. However, in the modern era, this rule must be seen in the light of the huge changes that have taken place with regard to pre-trial disclosure over the past 25 years.

For centuries, in the higher criminal courts at least, it was normal for the prosecution to inform the defendant of the nature of its case before trial, but the precise extent of this obligation was ill-defined. By contrast, the defendant was not normally required to disclose his or her case prior to trial. Over recent decades this has changed, as the investigation of crime has become increasingly complex. The prosecution now has a more clearly defined and extensive duty to set out its case and the evidence it will call, in advance of trial. However, defendants are also now required to state, in broad terms, the nature of their case and to indicate what prosecution evidence and assertions they accept. The introduction of evidence by formal admissions, made under section 10 CJA 1967, hitherto rare, is often actively encouraged, this occurring against a background of 'case management' pursuant to the provisions contained in the Criminal Procedure Rules (CPR) 2015 and the requirements of the Criminal Procedure and Investigations Act (CPIA) 1996. As a result, a defendant accused of insider dealing in the Crown Court will often have indicated what elements of the regulator's case he or she takes issue with prior to trial.

However, whether in advance of their hearing or at trial, it might be wise for more defendants to take issue with the highly technical prerequisites for committing the crime, even if the primary thrust of their defence lies elsewhere (ignorance of the alleged inside information, etc.).

The Indictment

The inherent nature of insider dealing prosecutions, the combined requirements of the Criminal Procedure Rules (CPR) and the Protocol on Complex Criminal Cases, along with the reluctance to see trials last longer than three months, necessarily encourage fairly 'activist' judges in such cases. Judges are often willing to insist that insider-dealing indictments are 'pruned' where they feel it necessary.[17]

David Kirk (Chief Criminal Counsel to the regulator from 2009 to 2013) has observed that in cases involving insider dealing 'rings' there will frequently be a large number of potential defendants. The natural preference of the prosecution will be for all of them to be tried together, so that the jury receives the entire 'picture'. However, in recent years, and to prevent trials becoming excessively long and complicated, judges have often been reluctant to see more than five (or even fewer) defendants in the dock at any one time, sometimes necessitating more than one hearing. Kirk has also noted that in many such prosecutions there will be a large number of alleged insider deals, whether they are indicted as a conspiracy or substantive counts. The regulator will want as many as possible to be covered in the evidence, both to demonstrate the gravity of the criminal activity and to rebut any suggestion that each accused person's success was merely a 'lucky'

---

17   Aleksandra Jordanoska, 'Case Management in Complex Fraud Trials: Actors and Strategies in Achieving Procedural Efficiency', 2017, p.343.

coincidence (commonly raised as part of a defence) or that the prosecution has been 'cherry-picking' trades. Again, in recent years it appears that some trial judges have sought to limit the number of counts/trades to be proved on an indictment, to ensure that the hearing remains manageable. Not uncommonly, it seems that the prosecution will be allowed to adduce evidence of up to six deals in any one indictment (a fairly arbitrary number).[18]

One judge in an insider trial subsequently observed: 'With Defendant X, I limited the number of stock lines that the prosecution could present to six, I think they were 21 or 23. If we had dealt with all of them we would still be doing the case now, it's impossible. The key case management issue is to restrict the prosecution to their best six tradings'.[19] However, neither of these trends (restrictions on the number of defendants and counts/trades) is a rigid rule.

Conspiracy or Substantive Offences?

As with many complex crimes, the prosecution will often have to make a choice as to whether to prosecute the insider dealing as a series of substantive offences (assuming there was more than one deal) or as one large conspiracy, contrary to Section 1 of the Criminal Law Act 1977 (CLA) — which makes it an offence to conspire to commit an act that would be a crime — or even as a series of conspiracies. All routes have their advantages, but only one type of count (for the same crime), can normally go to the jury, unless the prosecutor is able to justify a joint trial (very unusual). Indeed, judges will only rarely allow a trial to begin with both types of count, often being reluctant even to leave the choice of count to the close of the prosecution's case. Of course, this assumes that the insider is not also the dealer; conspiracy, by definition, needs at least two parties. Nevertheless, this is usually the case, as most insiders seek to place a layer between themselves and their trades.

In the early years of insider prosecutions under the CJA 1993, cases were often indicted as conspiracies, and this continues to be done with larger

---

18   David Kirk, 'Enforcement of Criminal Sanctions for Market Abuse: Practicalities, Problem Solving and Pitfalls', 2016, p.321.

19   Aleksandra Jordanoska, 'Case Management in Complex Fraud Trials: Actors and Strategies in Achieving Procedural Efficiency', 2017, p.343.

or more complex examples of such dealing.[20] Thus, in *R v Asif Nazir Butt* [2006] 2 Cr App R (S) 44, the five defendants were convicted of one count of conspiring to commit insider dealing contrary to section 52(1) of the CJA 1993 and section 1 of the CLA 1977. In this case, there had been 19 incidents of insider dealing over three years, as the primary defendant, whose work for an investment bank gave him access to confidential, price-sensitive inside information, passed information to his co-accused who dealt through accounts that they opened in their own names. In 2016, and as with *Butt*, the indictment in the huge trial of five men produced by the Operation Tabernula investigation contained a single count of conspiring to engage in insider dealing. By contrast, in 2013, a man was convicted of six counts of conspiracy to deal as an insider, with regard to six deals that actually took place. In this case, his alleged co-conspirator had moved to North Cyprus (which does not have an extradition agreement with the UK) prior to the trial.[21]

However, conspiracy counts present certain problems. Amongst them are that the prosecution must prove: the agreement; that the defendant knew what he or she was agreeing to; and that when he or she joined the agreement they intended that it be carried out. As a result, in recent years, the FSA/FCA has sometimes indicted for substantive offences, where a crime has been completed, each count normally being based on a specific insider trade, if the regulator concludes that these adequately reflect the gravity of what has occurred.

As the appeals in *R v Gray* (1995) 2 Cr App R 100 show, the decision to indict for conspiracy (or not) can significantly affect the evidence that can be adduced at trial. It should also be noted that where several separate (substantive) counts of insider dealing are present in the same indictment evidential issues might arise as to the extent to which they can support each other ('cross-admissibility') as incidents of 'bad character', because they show a propensity to offend in a certain manner, under section 101(1)(d) CJA 2003. Given the similarity of the offences this should not normally be

---

20   Paul Barnes, 'Insider Dealing and Market Abuse: The UK's Record on Enforcement', pp.174–189.

21   *Daily Telegraph*, 11 March 2013.

too problematic *provided* the jury is properly directed as to their use: *R v Chopra* [2007] 1 Cr App R 16.

Smoking Guns and Careless Defendants

An analysis of successful prosecutions brought by the FSA/FCA and other agencies for insider dealing since the start of the century show that the regulator (or other prosecutor) normally had either direct evidence, or the equivalent of something remarkably close to a 'smoking gun', such as circumstantial evidence of the most specific type. Furthermore, on close examination, many involved opportunistic defendants whose conduct appears acutely amateurish or at least inherently risky. Almost all cases involved accused persons who, even if generally careful, made serious errors at some point in the process. Although general circumstantial evidence was vital in 'setting the scene', stronger evidence was normally required to secure a conviction.

This pattern of careless mistakes in insider cases is found throughout the developed world. For example, in the USA, Bruce Carton, a former senior counsel in the SEC's Division of Enforcement, has noted that personal dealing by people whose firms are directly involved in merger transactions, or by those closely related to them (such as family members or 'significant others'), is still one of the most common mistakes seen in the field. This is so, he notes, even though it is the equivalent of someone robbing a bank while wearing a shirt with his name, address, and phone number written on it.[22]

This apparently crass error also regularly catches out insider dealers in the UK, despite numerous media reports revealing its dangers. For example, during the 2003 trial of an insider dealer who had traded under his own name, Philip Katz QC, prosecuting counsel, accused the defendant of being 'stupid' for this very reason. (He responded by suggesting that such conduct was indicative of his honesty).[23] Similarly, in 2015, a former senior executive was sentenced to a year's imprisonment when he pleaded guilty to two counts of insider dealing after buying shares in Ocado before

---

22 Bruce Carton, 'People, Please Stop Making these Two Insider-trading Mistakes!', *Compliance Week*, 29 July 2016.

23 *Daily Telegraph*, 23 January 2003.

its lucrative £216m tie-up with Morrisons was announced in 2013. A former Inland Revenue inspector, he had been at the centre of talks about the financial structure of the deal and its tax implications. He had also signed documents indicating that he was an 'insider' on the transaction and therefore restricted from dealing in connected shares. He then used two online accounts in the name of his long-term girlfriend (who was completely unaware of what he was doing) to buy and sell shares in Ocado between January 24 and May 17 2013, making a profit of £79,000 when they soared after the deal with Morrisons was announced.[24] It did not take much to connect him to the transaction.

In like manner, in early 2016, a former equities trader was sentenced to two years' in prison after pleading guilty to nine counts of insider trading spanning nine years from 2003, with his profits from the deals amounting to at least £155,162. He used inside information about significant corporate events, mainly mergers and acquisitions, to place share trades using accounts in his own name and those of (unknowing) close family members.[25] Similarly, at his hearing in late-2016, it was noted that Reshim Birk sometimes traded in the names of his wife and son (who were unaware of what was happening).[26]

By contrast, rogue-trading cells in which information is passed from the source to the dealer via several intermediaries are much harder to identify and prosecute. As a self-confessed insider dealer once observed: 'The more links in the chain, the more difficult it is to get caught. If you have some guy [trading] who is only tangentially connected or not connected at all [to the insider], how would the FSA [now the FCA] know?'[27]

Many more insider dealers have been caught out by their insistence on keeping formal records (whether paper or electronic) of their criminal trades, either because they are city professionals who cannot break the habits of a lifetime or because there is a perceived lack of 'honour amongst insider

---

24 *Daily Telegraph,* 3 March 2015.

25 *The Guardian,* 13 June 2016.

26 *Financial Times,* 29 November 2016.

27 Paul Barnes, 'Insider Dealing and Market Abuse: The UK's Record on Enforcement', 2011, pp.174–189.

dealers' and they fear being 'short-changed' by their colleagues. This fear is not entirely unjustified. In *Patel v Mirza* [2016] 3 W.L.R. 399 Mr Patel transferred £620,000 to Mr Mirza in order that the latter could trade shares on the basis of inside information about a bank. However, the transaction did not go through. Even so, the respondent kept the money and resisted Patel's claim for its return on the ground that it was barred for contractual illegality. (The Supreme Court ruled that a claimant who satisfied the ordinary requirements of a claim for unjust enrichment should not normally be debarred from enforcing his claim by reason only of the money, which he sought to recover, being paid for an unlawful purpose).

In other cases, some of those involved in offending have broken ranks and given evidence against their erstwhile colleagues, sometimes after active inducements were provided to them by the FSA/FCA (see below). Yet more have been careless about the manner in which they contacted each other, resorting to permanent (or at least preserved) written or employer recorded means of communication, even though private, 'out of office hours', verbal contact would have been just as effective, if a little less convenient.

All of these mistakes can be seen in recent successes on the part of the regulator, which, between the change in prosecution policy in 2008 and the end of 2016, secured 32 convictions (including guilty pleas) in relation to insider dealing, although many of them occurred in clusters arising from multi-handed trials.

The First Three Contested Cases

The first FSA insider dealing prosecution to produce a conviction, that involving Christopher McQuoid (a solicitor) and his father-in-law in March 2009, was a 'prosecutor's dream'. McQuoid was the General Counsel at TTP Communications Ltd. In May 2006, he was told in confidence that Motorola was planning to take over the company. Two days before the takeover was made public, his father-in-law bought 153,824 TTP shares, although he had not recently dealt in shares of any description, let alone of this type, or ever bought TTP shares before. This is important, as lawyers in such cases, whether for the prosecution or defence, usually familiarise themselves with the accused's previous trading patterns to determine whether the deals under investigation are consistent with past practice or 'out of character'. After the takeover of TTP Communications was publicly announced the swift rise in their share value meant that the father-in-law made a profit of £48,919.20 on selling them. Three months later, he gave his son-in-law a cheque for £24,459.60, exactly half of the profit to a penny.

Thus, this case involved a dealer with a clear and close personal link to the insider, with no active record of share dealing, purchases made in close proximity to the public announcement of price-sensitive information, an identifiable payment from dealer to insider, and with the icing on the cake being the near 'smoking gun' of the precise quantification of a half share of the profit made.

The second conviction from the 'new' era, in November 2009, involved the case of 24-year-old student Matthew Uberoi, who was on a six months' work experience scheme as an intern with stockbrokers Hoare Govett when he passed on price-sensitive information to his father. This led to his father purchasing shares in three companies, just before favourable announcements were made to the market, and then immediately selling them. In one case, he made a large profit, after purchasing 18,000 shares worth just over £90,000 in a small pharmaceutical company called Neutec Pharma, which was being advised by Matthew Uberoi's team at Hoare Govett. Shortly afterwards, Neutec announced that it was to be taken over by Swiss pharmaceutical company Novartis. The father was then able to sell his stake for close to £200,000. The other two purchases resulted in much smaller profits, the market failing to move very significantly when information was made public.

At trial, the jury was shown cryptic messages exchanged on a public web chat forum in which Matthew used an apparent code based on oriental restaurants to communicate with his father. He, the father, used the name BlueForever, while his son was known as Youthful Trader. In June 2006, Matthew sent a message to BlueForever saying: 'Let's have as much Chinese as we can. Today will be the last day we can do this ... all looks good on the Chinese front, think we should stock up'. BlueForever replied: 'Picked up another 3k this morning, cheers'. That morning, the father bought 3,000 shares in NeuTec Pharma. The next morning, Neutec announced the takeover offer from Novartis, which sent their share price soaring. Compounding his problems, the father's credit card statements showed that although he was a regular visitor to a Chinese restaurant in Croydon, his visits did not coincide with any talk of Chinese on the web forum.[28]

Uberoi's father was slightly better placed than Christopher McQuoid (see earlier in this chapter) had been. He was able to claim, quite plausibly, that he was 'completely addicted' to following the stock market and insisted he owed his share buying success to honest research on the Internet. Even better, he produced printouts from the Web relating to Neutec suggesting that it was widely seen as a good buy at the time. Despite this, his sudden predilection for the stocks of companies advised by his son's (effective) employer, together with his prescience in buying just prior to official announcements of good news, combined with the cryptic messages, meant that both men were convicted of 12 counts of insider trading conducted between June and August in 2006.

Obviously, it needed only the most cursory of examinations to link the insider to the dealer in this case. The messages sent via the Internet were also extremely unhelpful to the accused. The jury appears to have been influenced by the conjunction of such material with a number of allegations, over a relatively short period of time, perhaps working on the basis that: to invest in one firm in which your son has access to price-sensitive information is unlucky; two is carelessness; and three begins to look like insider dealing. Had Uberoi senior merely invested in the one very profitable deal and not exchanged electronic messages with his son (quite unnecessary in the circumstances), or, even better, had Uberoi junior used another (non-familial) dealer, the prospects for a conviction would have been greatly reduced.

The third successful prosecution involved Malcolm Calvert, a (retired) former partner at Cazenove stockbrokers, who used (and paid) a still undetected insider at his old firm to obtain information about a number of proposed mergers and takeovers between 2003 and 2005. He then passed details of these to his racing bookmaker and friend who, at his request, purchased shares in three companies: pharmaceutical group Vernalis; road-building business Johnston Group; and water company South Staffordshire. As a

---

result, three parties were involved in the insider dealing, albeit only two came for trial.

Calvert and his friend split the £103,000 profit from the illegal deals. They did not make the same mistakes as McQuoid. Calvert probably appreciated that, as a former employee of Cazenove, doing these deals personally would quickly arouse suspicion. Furthermore, the friend paid Calvert by leaving envelopes containing between £10,000 and £15,000 in cash with a bookmaker or at his (friend's) son's house for Calvert to collect. The jury took more than 18 hours to convict Calvert of five out of 12 counts of insider dealing. Nevertheless, and perhaps significantly, he was cleared on the remaining seven counts, relating to three more companies where Cazenove had advised on proposed deals.

In this case, the 'smoking gun' was to be the friend's willingness to break ranks and give evidence against his friend, without which any prosecution would have been impossible (as the prosecution freely conceded) in exchange for immunity from prosecution under SOCPA (see *Chapter 6*). By contrast, Calvert went to prison still refusing to give up his inside source at Cazenove.

The First Acquittal

The first FSA prosecution that failed to produce a single conviction occurred in May 2010, when a former finance director and two other men were acquitted of insider dealing. It was a revealing case. At the hearing, prosecuting counsel, Michael Bowes QC, alleged that the director had tipped off two of his friends (both of them solicitors), prior to a buyout of his company by a major Swiss pharmaceutical company. He categorically denied that he had leaked any information about the takeover to the pair, who had purchased a large amount of shares in the Swiss company shortly before the news was announced, each making a profit of £40,000. Thus, he was accused of a section 52(2) offence and his friends of a section 52(1) crime.

However, he suggested that it was merely his infectious enthusiasm for the business in which he worked that had been transmitted to his friends, without his giving them any specific information. He had simply told them he worked for a 'most amazing company' that would eventually make him a lot of money. This would plausibly explain why his two co-defendants would suddenly purchase an otherwise fairly obscure share.[29] After retiring for just 90 minutes the jury unanimously acquitted the men on all charges and they were awarded their costs. Although the case (like several others) expressly rejected the legal need for direct evidence of a statement being made, it shows that, in its absence, it can be difficult to establish that an alleged secondary insider was, in fact, prompted to deal by inside information, as opposed to other (entirely proper) factors.

The accused had quite legitimately made £3,000,000 from the sale of his own shares and stated in evidence that he was well-aware that the FSA was monitoring share movements in the company, both factors making it very unlikely that he would do anything improper. Most importantly, the two other defendants had made no attempt to conceal the deals or their relationship with him. As noted in the previous chapter, in practice this is often a crucial factor in successful prosecutions, because it makes it difficult to deny the presence of the essential elements of the case (knowledge, etc.) and suggests that the defendant appreciated that what he or she was doing was nefarious. Instead, as the jury must have clearly found, the defendants' account was entirely reasonable and convincing.[30]

Another Acquittal

Another case, this time from 2012, which produced acquittals for both of the accused who pleaded 'not guilty', is also revealing. A man who worked for a Japanese bank encouraged his two lovers (they were unaware of each other's existence) to invest in shares on his and their own behalf in a Dutch photocopier company after it was the subject of a takeover bid by Canon. Unusually, the trading took place long (up to nine months) before the acquisition occurred in November 2009. As a result, the two women concerned, a chiropractor, and wealthy mature student, eventually made more than £600,000 in profit. The man subsequently pleaded guilty to two counts of insider dealing (on his own behest) contrary to section 52(1), and two counts of encouraging insider dealing (by his lovers), contrary to section 52(2)(a) CJA 1993.

---

29 *The Times*, 26 May 2010.

30 *The Times*, 4 June 2010.

The two women who pleaded 'not guilty', were tried and acquitted of insider dealing contrary to section 52(1). The prosecution case was that they had agreed to give half of their profits to the man. However, both of them insisted that they had no idea at all that the advice he was giving them was based on inside information, rather than his own (widely acknowledged) financial shrewdness; that is, they denied an essential element of the offence, one that the prosecution had to prove beyond reasonable doubt. Moreover, they went further. One of the women also said she invested only after researching her lover's recommendation and personally calculating that the shares were undervalued, rather than relying on his advice. The other woman stated that he threatened to leave her unless she bought shares in the Dutch company, and that she did it purely to show that she loved and trusted him. As a result, both women raised a potential defence under section 53(1)(c), on the basis that they would have acted as they did without the inside information.[31]

Other Early FSA Cases

In many of the other 'early' insider dealing cases in which convictions were secured, whether after trial or by guilty pleas, the prosecutions were assisted by fundamental mistakes on the part of the accused persons. For example, although their operation was fairly sophisticated in some respects, in the 2011 trial of Christian and Angie Littlewood the Crown's work was greatly aided by the latter's habit of keeping quite detailed records of their criminal activity, many of which were recorded on a floppy disc kept hidden in the Littlewoods' garden shed. This yielded vital evidence when seized during a police raid, despite Christian's reported but unavailing attempt to destroy it as they entered his property with a search warrant. The disc contained, *inter alia*, spreadsheets identifying some trades and details of the cut each of them had received from others. The prosecution was also greatly assisted by Angie making large cash transfers from a bank account held under her Singaporean maiden name to both her husband and, more importantly, the dealer (Helmy Omar Sa'aid), and also by her dealing on her own account.[32]

---

31 *Daily Telegraph*, 15 November 2012.

32 *The Guardian*, 5 February 2011.

The disc could have been replaced by memory and trust, the bank transfers to Sa'aid by cash, while Angie could have refrained from dealing in a personal capacity.

Similarly, James Sanders, a City trader who pleaded guilty in 2012 after receiving inside tips from his sister-in-law in America, was partly convicted because investigators accessed 26 million emails and 24,000 automatically recorded and preserved telephone conversations at his Blue Index office. Several of these calls referred to deals based on tips he received from the USA, and in others Sanders openly dismissed the prospects of getting caught. Thus, on 30 October 2006, he spoke of getting information about an American accountancy firm who had: '... done the deal on a US company that's $23.77 at the moment and they're going to be bid for at $28 next week, 100 per cent so I'm going to do something quite big on it'. In another call, from April 2007, Sanders declared: 'There's no doubt in my mind we're gonna absolutely cane it over the next year or two because these tips are ****ing brilliant'.[33] None of these preserved communications were at all necessary.

It is not just electronic records and recordings that have proved disastrous for insider dealers. Graeme Shelley (see below), who pleaded guilty to the crime, appears to have maintained extensive handwritten notes of payments made to share the profits of their insider trading, notes that were discovered in his jacket pocket, the garment being hung in a cupboard and seized when he was arrested in March 2010. These records, which resembled a bookie's jottings, linked Rifat to various stock trades. Similar notes were later discovered in Rifat's desk at Moore Capital.[34]

Several other successful prosecutions involved defendants who sold shares they personally held in anticipation of bad news as a result of insider information they had received in a personal capacity. This will always be inherently dangerous, as the perpetrator is effortlessly linked to the deal, once a suspicious transaction has been flagged up. For example, in *R v Rollins* [2011] Crim LR 896, the senior manager of waste management company sold his entire shareholding, worth £174,000, in the group between August and September 2006, knowing that a publication of bad results in the latter

---

33   *The Independent*, 21 June 2012; *Daily Mail*, 20 June 2012; *Daily Mail*, 10 September 2012.

34   *Daily Telegraph*, 19 March 2015.

month was forthcoming. Just before the announcement, a memorandum had been circulated to senior management, including the appellant, warning about dealing when in possession of price-sensitive information. When the financial problems at the company were announced its share price dropped from 240p to about 140p per share. The manager's trading quickly came to the attention of the company's board of directors and he was summarily dismissed. Unsurprisingly, it also came to the attention of the authorities. He was convicted on five counts of insider dealing.[35]

Low Hanging Fruit

In 2007, Margaret Cole claimed that the FSA was focusing its efforts on insider dealing by City or business professionals who abused positions of trust by misusing information passed to them in their capacity as lawyers, accountants and brokers, especially where they were repeat offenders or making significant profits.[36] Despite this assertion, and unsurprisingly given the profiles of some of those initially prosecuted for insider dealing (see above), a persistent criticism of the FSA and its successor (the FCA) at this time was that they went after 'low hanging fruit', focusing on amateurish, and sometimes relatively small-scale, albeit readily provable operations, rather than sophisticated, high value, insider trading carried out by major 'players' in The Square Mile. This had always been a concern. Even in 1976, the City Company Law Committee had urged that the target of any new criminal offence should not be 'half-informed punters' but dishonest men who, by 'abusing a position of trust bet on a certainty'.[37] Almost 40 years later, a solicitor who represented one of those arrested in the Lodestone case went so far as to claim that: 'The FCA hasn't yet had a big scalp'.[38] Arguably, this deficiency was rectified in Operation Tabernula.

---

35   *Daily Telegraph*, 22 January 2011.

36   Speech by Margaret Cole to the American Bar Association, 4 October 2007.

37   Anon, *Insider Dealing*, 1976, p.2.

38   *Wall Street Journal*, UK edn., 4 January 2014.

Tabernula and other High Level Fruit

Operation Tabernula was the UK's largest ever insider trading investigation, taking almost nine years to complete, commencing under the FSA in 2007 and finishing with a major trial under its successor, the FCA, in 2016. Mark Steward, Director of Enforcement and Market Oversight at the latter body, described it as: '… an extraordinary and complex case of a type not prosecuted in this country before'. It was the first case of this type to make extensive use of covert evidence. It was also the first contested case of insider dealing since Operation Saturn in 2012 (which produced convictions for all but one of the seven defendants), although several individuals had pleaded guilty to the crime in the meantime.[39]

In Tabernula, it was also alleged that the convicted suspects manifested a high degree of 'professionalism' in their dealings, something that had often been missing in earlier cases. For example, the case allegedly involved the employment of hard to trace pay-as-you-go disposable mobile phones and the use of sophisticated encryption devices.

The investigation started with a suspicious transaction report (STR) filed with the FSA, after a trader risked £50,000 for every penny movement in Scottish & Newcastle shares, just ahead of a takeover announcement. It was ultimately claimed that the trader's remarkable confidence stemmed from information received from Martyn Dodgson, whose employer, Lehman Brothers, was advising Carlsberg on the deal, and who had access to documents referring to a minimum bid of 700p a share. As the regulator started examining this trade it led on to others, and it became apparent that several dealers were involved in a much wider scheme of questionable activity. The investigation only became public in March 2010, after 143 FSA staff, supported by officers from the Serious Organized Crime Agency (SOCA), carried out dawn raids on 16 addresses in London, Oxfordshire and Kent, arresting seven men in the process. It was SOCA's first involvement in an insider dealing case since its creation in 2006 and indicative of policing methods commonly associated with blue collar-crime now being employed for white-collar offences.[40] Three suspects, former L&G trader Paul Milsom,

---

39   *Financial Times*, 10 January 2016.

40   *The Times*, 24 March 2010.

Novum Securities' broker Graeme Shelley, and former Moore Capital trader Julian Rifat, pleaded guilty to various offences of insider dealing stemming from the investigation in 2013 and 2014 (their former employers were, of course, totally unaware of what occurred). However, the case only finished when two major City figures were convicted by majority verdict, and three men acquitted, in 2016, after long trials and a lengthy jury retirement.[41]

Martyn Dodgson, who received four-and-a-half years' imprisonment, the longest sentence for an insider dealing case ever awarded in the UK, was certainly a major figure in The Square Mile. A former senior broker at Deutsche Bank and Lehman Brothers, he had advised the government on bailed-out banks. Andrew Hind, the other man convicted in the trial, who received three-and-a-half years in prison, was a chartered accountant and former finance director at Topshop. The three acquitted defendants were a broker and two London day traders.

The FCA had accused Dodgson, who had access to documents on numerous price-sensitive deals while at *Deutsche Bank*, of passing inside information to Hind who then placed trades on their behalf through at least two of the others. It was alleged that £7.4m profit was made through trading on just six stocks. The three acquitted defendants vehemently denied any involvement in criminal activity and always stressed (where relevant) that they were completely unaware of the inside information when they traded, which deals they thought were based on the shrewd market analysis and business acumen of those eventually found guilty.

On Dodgson's key-ring investigators found the key for a red metal petty cash box, which had been discovered stashed under his bed at his home in Hampstead. Inside the box was a specialist encrypted storage drive called an IronKey, which its makers boasted was 'military grade'. Dodgson said he had not used the device in years and could not unlock it. It contained a drive with a 'self-destruct' mechanism that would erase data if the wrong password were entered ten times. However, by crosschecking other passwords, investigators were able to open the drive. The court was told that it contained incriminating evidence including a spreadsheet that listed coded

---

41   *Financial Times*, 6 May 2016.

references to the relevant trades. Once more, and despite all of Dodgson's 'professionalism', a penchant for recordkeeping had proved disastrous for insider dealers while, as in many similar cases, his generally 'suspicious' behaviour counted against him at trial.

Another high profile prosecution involving a sophisticated case and high level defendant was (rather belatedly) initiated in 2016, following the FCA's 'Operation Rye', when Mark Lyttleton, who had previously run a £2bn fund for the asset manager Blackrock, was charged with three counts of insider dealing between October and December 2011, albeit that the case ended in guilty pleas to two of them (the third count was dropped).

It was alleged that Lyttleton was able to use inside information to trade in shares in EnCore Oil PLC in October 2011, ahead of news being released about a proposed takeover of the company by Premier Oil and, a month later, to buy call options in Cairn Energy PLC after hearing of the results of a $600m exploration campaign to find oil and gas in the waters off Greenland, before it was released, something that caused its shares to drop the (fairly modest) total of one per cent.[42] Subsequently, the prosecution told the court that Lyttleton had executed the trades (while away from his employer's premises) through a Swiss firm using a Panamanian company seemingly set up under his (unknowing) wife's name. Use of offshore companies and bank accounts has long been a feature of the most sophisticated forms of insider dealing, as it can help disguise the money trail that leads up to a trade. As one observer noted in an entirely different context: 'You set up an offshore company in Belize, let's say, and maybe I use a bank in Malta or Gibraltar and I deal [in] the name of that company, there's no way they're going to find out who's behind that company'.[43] Perhaps unsurprisingly, given the complexity of the case, Lyttleton had been under investigation for almost three years before being charged.

42 *Financial Times*, 29 September 2016.

43 Paul Barnes, 'Insider Dealing and Market Abuse: The UK's Record on Enforcement', 2011, pp.174–189.

CHAPTER 8

Conclusion

Introduction

Following sharp price movements in HBOS shares in March 2008, Lord Stevenson (then the company's chairman) complained that there was strong reason for believing that the UK was 'exceptionally bad at dealing with white-collar crime. Only two weeks ago I was in New York and two people were convicted of insider dealing. We appear not to pursue things in the same way'.[1] Just a year later, there had been a sea change, and the regulator had instigated a rash of prosecutions. As a result, in March 2009, Hector Sants, the authority's chief executive, felt able to announce that people should be 'very frightened of the FSA'.[2]

Arguably, engendering this level of anxiety requires the threat of criminal, not merely civil, sanctions, as the latter are much less likely to produce 'life-changing' consequences for their recipients. It is a cliché, but nevertheless probably true, that white-collar criminals fear custody more than other offenders, while it is sometimes argued that the risk of purely financial penalties, imposed under a regulatory regime, simply becomes just another business overhead, to be factored in to deal-making (suspension from trading is, of course, another matter). In the Australian case of *R v Curtis* (No.3) [2016] NSWSC 866, Justice McCallum stated that the risk

---

1   *The Guardian*, 27 June 2008.
2   *Financial Times*, 12 March 2009.

of custody, provided it was real, was an effective deterrent for insider deal-ers, because: 'White-collar crime is a field in which, perhaps more than any other, offending is often a choice freely made by well-educated people from privileged backgrounds, prompted by greed rather than the more pernicious influences of poverty, mental illness or addiction'. Empirical research in a variety of countries also suggests that simply drafting anti-insider dealing laws is not associated with greatly cleaner markets. It is the active enforce-ment of such laws that brings this about.[3]

In recent years, and partly under the pressure of external events, the FSA/ FCA has transformed section 52 of the CJA 1993 from a rarely used provi-sion into a fairly regularly and effectively used one in terms of prosecutions. Insider dealers now face the risk of a significant period of imprisonment, something that barely featured in their calculations in the 1990s. The era of safe (from criminal prosecution), highly remunerative, but essentially 'amateur' insider dealing is past. In early-2017, Mark Steward, the FCA's executive director of enforcement and market oversight, was undoubtedly correct when he observed that insider dealers were 'more likely to be caught than ever before'.

Nevertheless, the current prosecution regime is still unlikely to be suc-cessful against sophisticated insider dealers *provided* that they are extremely careful, and are not unlucky enough to be made an 'example' of by an FCA that is willing to invest the enormous resources often needed to satisfy the demanding criminal standard of proof.

'Successful' Insider Dealing

From what we can conclude after an examination of the reported cases and other data, an insider is unlikely to be prosecuted to conviction if:

- he or she selects a tough-minded and reliable dealer to conduct the trades, one with whom they have minimal contact, such as a friend from early on in life who has revived their acquaintanceship many years later;

---

3   Utpal Bhattacharya and Hazem Daouk, 'The World Price of Insider Trading', 2002, p.104.

- (ideally) there is at least one further layer in the chain between insider and dealer;
- all communications between the two (or more) are oral and made face-to-face in an open space such as a park, rather than by telephone in potentially 'bugged' premises;
- their meetings are kept to a minimum;
- share purchases are made relatively early, perhaps when a price-sensitive management decision appears (very) likely rather than certain, and only made occasionally;
- payments to the insider are always in cash or gifts and made months after the trade, in a series of small amounts, perhaps with a pretext being manufactured for use in an emergency (such as payment for the purchase of an antique);
- the dealer actively trades in shares, particularly in the relevant field and, on the day he or she dealt in the insider shares, had made a major purchase of other equities to serve as a 'blind';
- the dealer has conducted some 'research' into the relevant share, printing off some generally supportive (and provably dated) financial journalism, from the huge amount available in the modern era, explaining why his or her attention should suddenly have turned to the relevant company; and
- finally, the dealer and insider do not keep any written or electronic records of what occurred, relying purely on memory and trust to divide profits.

However, being extremely cautious adds enormously to the time and care that has to be taken in these cases and greatly reduces the financial returns available from such criminal activity. It is also inherently quite difficult for some of these precautions to be met. Most insiders would find it hard to find 'reliable' dealers with whom they have had minimal previous social contact. Furthermore, even for the most careful operators, it is extremely difficult to deal as an insider on a regular basis without eventually making mistakes, as Operation Tabernula demonstrated (see *Chapter 7*). Additionally, insider dealing puts the insider permanently at the mercy of the dealer (and vice-versa). Not many people would wish to have this hanging over them.

Criminal prosecutions are clearly not a panacea for insider dealing; they can never deter all or even most cases. The odds against exposure remain too good. According to some empirical studies there are 1,000 instances of significant insider dealing a year in the UK. This compares with, on average, perhaps three criminal prosecutions annually, so that the chances of being caught are still in the region of one in 300.[4] (Other assessments would place the number of important inside deals at a lower level).

However, it must always be remembered that most prosecuted insider dealers have a great deal to lose, so that even a comparatively modest level of threat will carry far more weight than it would with many 'conventional' offenders. Of course, such crimes are not always based solely on greed, despite regular judicial suggestions to the contrary. According to the psychologist Douglas Hirschhorn, they are also: '… about winning. About finding an advantage and beating your competitors'.[5] Nevertheless, with this caveat, most high-level individuals who are in receipt of price-sensitive information are already extremely well paid professionals and such people make up the majority of insider prosecution defendants, although cases involving inquisitive support staff provide periodic exceptions to this general pattern.

For example, Julian Rifat may have made £285,000 from insider trading but he was (reportedly) earning in the region of £700,000 a year in salary at Moore Capital.[6] Martyn Dodgson made substantial sums from insider dealing but was (allegedly) paid about £600,000 a year as a managing director at Deutsche Bank. In one of the most extreme cases, Mark Lyttleton made just £35,000 pounds from insider trading, at a time when it seems he was earning a very large salary at Blackrock. Their convictions did not merely cost them their liberty, but in many cases their careers, incomes, professional status, reputations and future ability to work in The Square Mile.

---

4   Paul Barnes, 'Insider Dealing and Market Abuse: The UK's Record on Enforcement', 2011, pp.174–189.

5   *The Guardian*, 5 February 2011.

6   *Financial Times*, 19 May 2016.

Success

As a result, and despite their inherent difficulty and expense, it seems that even occasional prosecutions, if only *pour encourager les autres*, have had a significant impact on the incidence of insider dealing. After remaining close to 30 per cent for four years, the FCA's market cleanliness statistic (which measures suspicious trades) for takeovers decreased to about 15 per cent in the years between 2010 and 2013. Significantly, this decline began in the final quarter of 2009, so that it coincides closely with, and was *probably* spawned by, the increase in criminal prosecutions and convictions at this time.[7] Unsurprisingly, in these circumstances, in 2012 the FCA's Director of Enforcement and Financial Crime said that the new 'tough approach' towards insider dealing would continue.

Even so, in subsequent years the FCA had to focus much of its limited resources on various benchmark-rigging probes, such as that pertaining to the London Interbank Offered Rate (LIBOR).[8] This may have been at least partly at the expense of insider dealing investigations and prosecutions, which appear to have declined. Perhaps significantly, in the early-summer of 2016, the FCA revealed that abnormal movements in share prices ahead of public announcement of takeovers were at their highest level for five years, albeit still well below pre-2010 rates. In 2015 and 2016 they stood at about 19 per cent. This raised the possibility that such an increase could have been the side-effect of a dearth of well-publicised prosecutions over the previous few years, which might otherwise have had a deterrent effect on potential insider traders.[9] Of course, it is also possible that they may simply have adjusted to the new environment by becoming more sophisticated in their dealings.

Nevertheless, it is clear that the FCA is determined not to return to the situation that prevailed prior to 2008, as can be seen from the large number of investigations opened in 2016 and 2017. These increased from eight cases in 2014/5 to 22 cases in 2015/16, while 14 cases were opened between 1

---

7   Jim Goldman *et al*, '*Why Has the FCA's Market Cleanliness Statistic for Takeover Announcements Decreased Since 2009?*', 2014, p.24.

8   *Financial Times*, 10 January 2016.

9   *Financial Times*, 29 September 2016; *The Times*, 6 July 2017.

April and 31 July 2016 alone.[10] Some were extremely largescale. In November 2016, it was reported that, over the previous few months, the National Crime Agency (which replaced the Serious and Organized Crime Agency (SOCA) in 2013) had arrested three employees from blue-chip banks as part of a major UK insider trading investigation linked to the 'Panama Papers' (the leak of information from an international law firm based in the central American country) in an operation led by the FCA.[11] This active approach shows the continuing faith the regulator places in the ability of criminal prosecutions to influence behaviour in the financial services industry.

Concern

Despite such (apparent) success, there has also been a slightly more unsettling side to the expansion of the criminal process in insider cases over recent years. Understandably, those accused of this crime do not attract much popular sympathy, especially since the economic crisis of 2008. Many would agree with Margaret Cole that they are criminals in suits masquerading as city professionals.[12] Perhaps, in part, because of this, the courts have allowed the provisions contained in the CJA 1993 to be pushed to their limit in recent years, as the Statute is viewed through the prism of the financial crisis. This has meant that obvious ambiguities in the legislation have often been quietly ignored, being 'flexibly' interpreted in the light of the mischief that the Statute was aimed at counteracting. This might, eventually, occasion a miscarriage of justice and also, perhaps, establish a bad precedent for others accused of socially unpopular crimes.

Arguably, it is time for a fourth attempt at drafting a crime of insider dealing, one that is appropriate to the Internet age, while defence counsel in such cases might be well-advised to be more willing to question whether elements of the offence have always been made out, even if they are denying any involvement by their lay clients in what has occurred. This might also lead to some much-needed guidance on the Statute from the Court of Appeal.

Furthermore, successful investigations into insider dealing have the

---

10   *Money Marketing*, 23 September 2016.

11   *The Guardian*, 11 November 2016.

12   *The Lawyer*, 13 June 2010.

potential to be highly intrusive, frequently requiring intense surveillance of suspects and a breach of their privacy. For some observers, this may be entirely acceptable when it comes to dealing with crimes such as terrorism and largescale Class A drug importation, but occasions a degree of concern when used for something that was entirely legal (if improper) as recently as the end of the 1970s.

Such commentators might argue that it is significant that the move towards charging insider dealing as a crime, which was largely driven by the financial crisis, has occurred even as Deferred Prosecution Agreements (DPAs) have been introduced by the Crime and Courts Act 2013, aimed at avoiding criminal prosecutions for corporate bodies suspected of fraudulent activity, in exchange for civil penalties, such as payment of a fine and compensation to victims, and the introduction of procedures to prevent re-offending. Some of them might suggest that it would be better for the FCA to focus on its potent, and much more easily established, regulatory powers, a few high profile, readily provable, and well-publicised criminal cases apart, on the basis that it is certainty, rather than gravity, of punishment that best deters offending. The money saved on criminal cases could then be used in funding improved preventative training and education for financial institutions (the regulator has long advised on good practice in handling inside information) and furthering the FCA's existing focus on the systems and controls used by firms to prevent market abuse.

Ultimately, everything turns on how seriously the crime is viewed, and this is something about which there is, and always has been, a huge variety of opinion; which is almost where this little book began.

Part V Criminal Justice Act 1993 (as amended)

The offence of insider dealing

52 The offence

(1) An individual who has information as an insider is guilty of insider dealing if, in the circumstances mentioned in subsection (3), he deals in securities that are price-affected securities in relation to the information.

(2) An individual who has information as an insider is also guilty of insider dealing if—

   (a)   he encourages another person to deal in securities that are (whether or not that other knows it) price-affected securities in relation to the information, knowing or having reasonable cause to believe that the dealing would take place in the circumstances mentioned in subsection (3); or

   (b)   he discloses the information, otherwise than in the proper performance of the functions of his employment, office or profession, to another person.

(3) The circumstances referred to above are that the acquisition or disposal in question occurs on a regulated market, or that the person

dealing relies on a professional intermediary or is himself acting as a professional intermediary.

(4) This section has effect subject to section 53.

53 Defences

(1) An individual is not guilty of insider dealing by virtue of dealing in securities if he shows—

  (a) that he did not at the time expect the dealing to result in a profit attributable to the fact that the information in question was price-sensitive information in relation to the securities, or

  (b) that at the time he believed on reasonable grounds that the information had been disclosed widely enough to ensure that none of those taking part in the dealing would be prejudiced by not having the information, or

  (c) that he would have done what he did even if he had not had the information.

(2) An individual is not guilty of insider dealing by virtue of encouraging another person to deal in securities if he shows—

  (a) that he did not at the time expect the dealing to result in a profit attributable to the fact that the information in question was price-sensitive information in relation to the securities, or

  (b) that at the time he believed on reasonable grounds that the information had been or would be disclosed widely enough to ensure that none of those taking part in the dealing would be prejudiced by not having the information, or

  (c) that he would have done what he did even if he had not had the information.

(3) An individual is not guilty of insider dealing by virtue of a disclosure of information if he shows—

(a) that he did not at the time expect any person, because of the disclosure, to deal in securities in the circumstances mentioned in subsection (3) of section 52; or

(b) that, although he had such an expectation at the time, he did not expect the dealing to result in a profit attributable to the fact that the information was price-sensitive information in relation to the securities.

(4) Schedule 1 (special defences) shall have effect.

(5) The Treasury may by order amend Schedule 1.

(6) In this section references to a profit include references to the avoidance of a loss.

Interpretation

54 Securities to which Part V applies

(1) This Part applies to any security which—

(a) falls within any paragraph of Schedule 2; and

(b) satisfies any conditions applying to it under an order made by the Treasury for the purposes of this subsection; and in the provisions of this Part (other than that Schedule) any reference to a security is a reference to a security to which this Part applies.

(2) The Treasury may by order amend Schedule 2.

55 'Dealing' in securities

(1) For the purposes of this Part, a person deals in securities if—

(a) he acquires or disposes of the securities (whether as principal or agent); or

(b) he procures, directly or indirectly, an acquisition or disposal of the securities by any other person.

(2) For the purposes of this Part, *'acquire'*, in relation to a security, includes—

(a) agreeing to acquire the security; and

(b) entering into a contract which creates the security

(3) For the purposes of this Part, *'dispose'*, in relation to a security, includes—

(a) agreeing to dispose of the security; and

(b) bringing to an end a contract which created the security.

(4) For the purposes of subsection (1), a person procures an acquisition or disposal of a security if the security is acquired or disposed of by a person who is—

(a) his agent,

(b) his nominee, or

(c) a person who is acting at his direction, in relation to the acquisition or disposal.

(5) Subsection (4) is not exhaustive as to the circumstances in which one person may be regarded as procuring an acquisition or disposal of securities by another.

56 'Inside information', etc.

(1) For the purposes of this section and section 57, *'inside information'* means information which—

(a) relates to particular securities or to a particular issuer of securities or to particular issuers of securities and not to securities generally or to issuers of securities generally;

(b) is specific or precise;

(c) has not been made public; and

(d) if it were made public would be likely to have a significant effect on the price of any securities.

(2) For the purposes of this Part, securities are *price-affected securities* in relation to inside information, and inside information is *price-sensitive information* in relation to securities, if and only if the information would, if made public, be likely to have a significant effect on the price of the securities.

(3) For the purposes of this section *price* includes value.

57 'Insiders

(1) For the purposes of this Part, a person has information as an insider if and only if—

  (a) it is, and he knows that it is, inside information, and

  (b) he has it, and knows that he has it, from an inside source.

(2) For the purposes of subsection (1), a person has information from an inside source if and only if—

  (a) he has it through—

      (i) being a director, employee or shareholder of an issuer of securities; or

      (ii) having access to the information by virtue of his employment, office or profession; or

  (b) the direct or indirect source of his information is a person within paragraph (a).

58 Information 'made public'

(1) For the purposes of section 56, *made public*, in relation to information, shall be construed in accordance with the following provisions of this section; but those provisions are not exhaustive as to the meaning of that expression.

(2) Information is made public if—

  (a) it is published in accordance with the rules of a regulated market for the purpose of informing investors and their professional advisers;

(b)   it is contained in records which by virtue of any enactment are open to inspection by the public;

(c)   it can be readily acquired by those likely to deal in any securities—

(i)   to which the information relates, or

(ii) of an issuer to which the information relates; or

(d)   it is derived from information which has been made public.

(3) Information may be treated as made public even though—

(a)   it can be acquired only by persons exercising diligence or expertise;

(b)   it is communicated to a section of the public and not to the public at large;

(c)   it can be acquired only by observation;

(d)   it is communicated only on payment of a fee; or

(e)   it is published only outside the United Kingdom.

59 'Professional intermediary'

(1) For the purposes of this Part, a 'professional intermediary' is a person—

(a)   who carries on a business consisting of an activity mentioned in subsection (2) and who holds himself out to the public or any section of the public (including a section of the public constituted by persons such as himself) as willing to engage in any such business; or

(b)   who is employed by a person falling within paragraph (a) to carry out any such activity.

(2) The activities referred to in subsection (1) are—

(a)   acquiring or disposing of securities (whether as principal or agent); or

(b)   acting as an intermediary between persons taking part in any dealing in securities.

(3) A person is not to be treated as carrying on a business consisting of an activity mentioned in subsection (2)—

(a) if the activity in question is merely incidental to some other activity not falling within subsection (2); or

(b) merely because he occasionally conducts one of those activities.

(4) For the purposes of section 52, a person dealing in securities relies on a professional intermediary if and only if a person who is acting as a professional intermediary carries out an activity mentioned in subsection (2) in relation to that dealing.

60 Other interpretation provisions

(1) For the purposes of this Part, *'regulated market'* means any market, however operated, which, by an order made by the Treasury, is identified (whether by name or by reference to criteria prescribed by the order) as a regulated market for the purposes of this Part.

(2) For the purposes of this Part an *'issuer'*, in relation to any securities, means any company, public sector body or individual by which or by whom the securities have been or are to be issued.

(3) For the purposes of this Part—

(a) *'company'* means any body (whether or not incorporated and wherever incorporated or constituted) which is not a public sector body; and

(b) *'public sector body'* means—

(i) the government of the United Kingdom, of Northern Ireland or of any country or territory outside the United Kingdom;

(ii) a local authority in the United Kingdom or elsewhere;

(iii) any international organisation the members of which include the United Kingdom or another member state;

(iv) the Bank of England; or

(v) the central bank of any sovereign State.

(4) For the purposes of this Part, information shall be treated as relating to an issuer of securities which is a company not only where it is about the company but also where it may affect the company's business prospects.

Miscellaneous

61 Penalties and prosecution

(1) An individual guilty of insider dealing shall be liable—

   (a) on summary conviction, to a fine not exceeding the statutory maximum or imprisonment for a term not exceeding six months or to both; or

   (b) on conviction on indictment, to a fine or imprisonment for a term not exceeding seven years or to both.

(2) Proceedings for offences under this Part shall not be instituted in England and Wales except by or with the consent of—

   (a) the Secretary of State; or

   (b) the Director of Public Prosecutions.

(3) In relation to proceedings in Northern Ireland for offences under this Part, subsection (2) shall have effect as if the reference to the Director of Public Prosecutions were a reference to the Director of Public Prosecutions for Northern Ireland.61A.— Summary proceedings: venue and time limit for proceedings

62 Territorial scope of offence of insider dealing

(1) An individual is not guilty of an offence falling within subsection (1) of section 52 unless—

   (a) he was within the United Kingdom at the time when he is alleged to have done any act constituting or forming part of the alleged dealing;

   (b) the regulated market on which the dealing is alleged to have occurred is one which, by an order made by the Treasury, is identified (whether by name or by reference to criteria prescribed by the order) as being, for the purposes of this Part, regulated in the United Kingdom; or

(c) the professional intermediary was within the United Kingdom at the time when he is alleged to have done anything by means of which the offence is alleged to have been committed.

(2) An individual is not guilty of an offence falling within subsection (2) of section 52 unless—

(a) he was within the United Kingdom at the time when he is alleged to have disclosed the information or encouraged the dealing; or

(b) the alleged recipient of the information or encouragement was within the United Kingdom at the time when he is alleged to have received the information or encouragement.

63 Limits on section 52

(1) Section 52 does not apply to anything done by an individual acting on behalf of a public sector body in pursuit of monetary policies or policies with respect to exchange rates or the management of public debt or foreign exchange reserves.

(2) No contract shall be void or unenforceable by reason only of section 52.

SCHEDULE 2

Securities

Shares

1   Shares and stock in the share capital of a company ('shares').

Debt securities

2   Any instrument creating or acknowledging indebtedness which is issued by a company or public sector body, including, in particular,

debentures, debenture stock, loan stock, bonds and certificates of deposit ('debt securities').

Warrants

3   Any right (whether conferred by warrant or otherwise) to subscribe for shares or debt securities ('warrants').

Depositary receipts

4   (1) The rights under any depositary receipt.

(2) For the purposes of sub-paragraph (1) a 'depositary receipt' means a certificate or other record (whether or not in the form of a document)—

   (a)   which is issued by or on behalf of a person who holds any relevant securities of a particular issuer; and
   (b)   which acknowledges that another person is entitled to rights in relation to the relevant securities or relevant securities of the same kind.

(3) In sub-paragraph (2) 'relevant securities' means shares, debt securities and warrants.

Options

5   Any option to acquire or dispose of any security falling within any other paragraph of this Schedule.

Futures

6   (1) Rights under a contract for the acquisition or disposal of relevant securities under which delivery is to be made at a future date and at a price agreed when the contract is made.

(2) In sub-paragraph (1)—

(a) the references to a future date and to a price agreed when the contract is made include references to a date and a price determined in accordance with terms of the contract; and

(b) 'relevant securities' means any security falling within any other paragraph of this Schedule.

Contracts for differences

7 (1) Rights under a contract which does not provide for the delivery of securities but whose purpose or pretended purpose is to secure a profit or avoid a loss by reference to fluctuations in —

(a) a share index or other similar factor connected with relevant securities;

(b) the price of particular relevant securities; or

(c) the interest rate offered on money placed on deposit.

(2) In sub-paragraph (1) 'relevant securities' means any security falling within any other paragraph of this Schedule.

Frequently Used Acronyms

AIM	Alternative Investment Market
CEP	Complex event processing
CFD	Contract for difference
CJA	Criminal Justice Act
CSMAD	Criminal Sanctions for Market Abuse Directive
CPR	Criminal Procedure Rules
CPS	Crown Prosecution Service
DPA	Deferred prosecution agreement
DTI	Department of Trade and Industry
ECHR	European Convention on Human Rights
EFCD	Enforcement and Financial Crime Division
EMOD	Enforcement and Market Oversight Division
FEMR	*Fair and Effective Markets Review*
FCA	Financial Conduct Authority
FSA	Financial Services Authority
FSMA	Financial Services and Markets Act 2000
HRA	Human Rights Act 1998
LSE	London Stock Exchange
MAR	Market Abuse Regulation 2016
MAD	Market Abuse Directive
MDP	Market data processor
OTC	Over-the-counter
PACE	Police and Criminal Evidence Act 1984

POCA	Proceeds of Crime Act 2002
PRA	Prudential Regulation Authority
RIPA	Regulation of Investigatory Powers Act 2000
RNS	Regulatory News Service
SEC	Securities and Exchange Commission (USA)
SFO	Serious Fraud Office
SOCA	Serious Organized Crime Agency
SOCPA	Serious Organized Crime and Police Act 2005
STOR	Suspicious transaction and order report
STR	Suspicious transaction report

Select Bibliography

Alexander, Kern (2001) *Insider Dealing and Market Abuse: The Financial Services and Markets Act 2000,* ESRC Centre for Business Research, Working Paper No. 222, Cambridge.

Anderson, Geraint (2009) *Cityboy: Beer and Loathing in the Square Mile,* Headline, London.

Anderson, Karen *et al* (2017) *A Practitioner's Guide to the Law and Regulation of Market Abuse,* 2nd edn., Sweet & Maxwell, London.

Anon (1976) *Insider Dealing,* City Company Law Committee Report, London. Held by Bodleian Law Library (at KN 304.9 CIT 1979).

Barnard, Jonathan (2011) 'Insider Trading: An Easy Offence To Commit', Cloth Fair Chambers, London.

Barnes, Paul (2009) *Stock Market Efficiency, Insider Dealing and Market Abuse,* Routledge, London.

Barnes, Paul (2011) 'Insider Dealing and Market Abuse: The UK's Record on Enforcement', *International Journal of Law, Crime and Justice,* Vol. 39, pp.174–189.

Bhattacharya, Utpal and Daouk, Hazem, (2002) 'The World Price of Insider Trading', *Journal of Finance,* Vol. 57, No. 1, pp.75–108.

Braggion, F and Moore, L (2013) 'How Insiders Traded Before Rules', *Business History,* Vol. 55, pp.565–584.

Bromberg, Lev *et al* (2017) 'The Extent and Intensity of Insider Trading Enforcement — An International Comparison', *Journal of Corporate Law Studies,* Vol. 17, Issue 1, pp.73–110.

Cheung, Rita (2010) 'Criminal Prosecution for Insider Dealing: A Hong Kong Perspective', *Company Lawyer*, Vol. 31, pp.160–164.

Clarke, Sarah (2013) *Insider Dealing: Law and Practice*, Oxford University Press, Oxford.

Copi, Irving (1953) *Introduction to Logic*, Macmillan, London.

Davies, Jack (2015) 'From Gentlemanly Expectations to Regulatory Principles: A History of Insider Dealing in the UK (Pt.1)', *Company Lawyer*, Vol. 36(5), pp.132–143.

Davies, Jack (2015) 'From Gentlemanly Expectations to Regulatory Principles: A History of Insider Dealing in the UK (Pt.2)', *Company Lawyer*, Vol. 36(6), pp.163–174.

Dumez, Herve (2016) 'The Description of the First Financial Market: Looking Back on Confusion of Confusions by Joseph de la Vega', Gerer & Comprendre, No. 1, pp.5–9.

Estevan de Quesada, Carmen (2014) 'Regulatory Models of Insider Trading and the Concept of "Use of Inside Information"', *Law and Forensic Science*, Vol. 7, pp.169–191.

Filby, Michael (2003) 'The Enforcement of Insider Dealing Under the Financial Services and Markets Act 2000', *Company Lawyer*, Vol. 24(11), pp.334–351.

Fisher, Jonathan (2010) 'Fighting Fraud and Financial Crime: A New Architecture for the Investigation and Prosecution of Serious Fraud, Corruption and Financial Market Crimes', Policy Exchange Research Note, London.

Fisher, Jonathan (2013) 'Who Should Prosecute Fraud, Corruption and Financial Markets Crime?' London School of Economics, Law and Financial Markets Project, Briefing 3/13, http://www.lse.ac.uk/law/Assets/Documents/law-and-financial-markets-project/fisher-who-should-prosecute.pdf

Goldman, Jim *et al* (2014) 'Why Has the FCA's Market Cleanliness Statistic for Takeover Announcements Decreased Since 2009?', FCA Occasional Papers in Financial Regulation, London.

Goodhart, William *et al* (1972) *Insider Trading: A Report by Justice*, Justice, London.

Hamer, David (2007) 'The Presumption of Innocence and Reverse Burdens: A Balancing Act', *Cambridge Law Journal*, Vol. 66, pp.142–171.

Hannigan, Brenda (1994) *Insider Dealing*, 2nd edn., Longman, London.

Harrison, Karen and Ryder, Nicholas (2013) *The Law Relating to Financial Crime in the United Kingdom*, Routledge, London.

Jordanoska, Aleksandra (2017) 'Case Management in Complex Fraud Trials: Actors and Strategies in Achieving Procedural Efficiency', *International Journal of Law in Context*, Vol. 13, Issue 3, pp.336–355.

Kirk, David (2016) 'Enforcement of Criminal Sanctions for Market Abuse: Practicalities, Problem Solving and Pitfalls', *ERA Forum*, Vol. 17(3), pp.311–322.

Macey, Jonathan R (1999) 'Securities Trading: A Contractual Perspective', *Case Western Reserve Law Review*, Vol. 50, pp.269–290.

Marshall, H H (1978), 'Insider Trading', *The International and Comparative Law Quarterly*, Vol. 27, No. 1, pp.250–252.

McDonnell, Brian (2012) *A Practitioner's Guide to Inside Information*, 2nd edn., Sweet & Maxwell, London.

Montgomery, Clare *et al* (eds.) (2015) *Fraud: Criminal Law and Procedure*, Oxford University Press, Oxford.

Quo, Shirley (2017) 'The Moral Ambiguity of Insider Trading as a White-collar Crime', *Company Lawyer*, Vol. 38(7), pp.203–213

Rider, Barry *et al* (2016) *Market Abuse and Insider Dealing*, 3rd edn., Bloomsbury Professional, London.

Rider, Barry and French, H Leigh (1979) *The Regulation of Insider Trading*, Macmillan, London.

Seredyńska, Iwona (2012) *Insider Dealing and Criminal Law: Dangerous Liaisons*, Springer, London.

Thompson, James H (2013) 'A Global Comparison of Insider Trading Regulations', *International Journal of Accounting and Financial Reporting*, Vol. 3, no. 1, pp.1–23.

Wilson, Gary and Wilson, Sarah (2014) 'The FSA, 'Credible Deterrence', and Criminal Enforcement: A "Haphazard Pursuit?"', *Journal of Financial Crime*, Vol. 21(1), pp.4–28.

Wilson, Sarah (2014) *The Origins of Modern Financial Crime: Historical*

Foundations and Current Problems in Britain, Routledge, London.

Wotherspoon, Keith (1994) 'Insider Dealing: The New Law: Part V of the Criminal Justice Act 1993', *Modern Law Review*, Vol. 57, No. 3, pp.419–433.

Index

Fields, Fens and Felonies

Crime and Justice in Eighteenth-Century East Anglia
Gregory J Durston

It was a time of highwaymen, footpads and
desperate petty offenders, draconian penalties,
extremes of wealth and poverty, corruption
and rough and emerging forms of justice. A
fascinating and absorbing account of crimes,
responses and penal outcomes of the era.

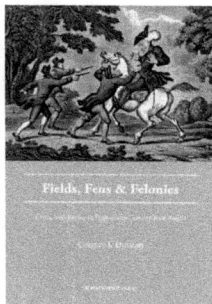

Paperback & Ebook | ISBN 978-1-909976-11-5 | 2016 | 736 pages

Whores and Highwaymen

Crime and Justice in the Eighteenth-Century Metropolis
Gregory J Durston

The 'whores' and 'highwaymen' of Gregory Durston's
title are just some of the dubious characters met
with in this fascinating work, including thief-takers,
trading justices, an upstart legal profession whose
lower orders developed various ways to line their own
pockets and magistrates and clerks who preferred
dealing with those cases which attracted fees.

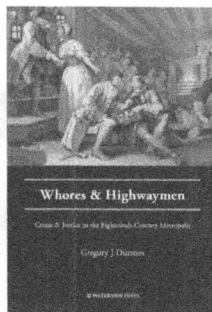

'A very-well-researched and readable
book…a bit of a romp'—*The Law Society Gazette*

Hardback, Paperback & Ebook | ISBN 978-1-909976-39-9 | 2016 | 672 pages

www.WatersidePress.co.uk